Introducing Philosophy

To the students of my introductory classes,
1966–96

Also by D. Z. Phillips

The Concept of Prayer
Faith and Philosophical Enquiry
Death and Immortality
Moral Practices (with H. O. Mounce)
Sense and Delusion (with Ilham Dilman)
Athronyddu am Grefydd
Religion Without Explanation
Dramau Gwenlyn Parry
Through a Darkening Glass
Belief, Change and Forms of Life
R. S. Thomas: Poet of the Hidden God
From Fantasy to Faith
Interventions in Ethics
Wittgenstein and Religion
Writers of Wales: J. R. Jones

Introducing Philosophy

The Challenge of Scepticism

D. Z. Phillips

BLACKWELL
Publishers

First published 1996
Reprinted 1997

Blackwell Publishers Ltd
108 Cowley Road
Oxford OX4 1JF, UK

Blackwell Publishers Inc
350 Main Street
Malden, Massachusetts 02148, USA

British Library Cataloguing in Publication Data
A CIP catalogue record for this book is available from the British Library

Library of Congress Cataloging in Publication Data
Phillips, D. Z. (Dewi Zephaniah)
Introducing philosophy : the challenge of scepticism / D. Z. Phillips.
p. cm.
Includes bibliographical references and index.
ISBN 0–631–20040–1 (hbk : alk. paper)
ISBN 0–631–20041–X (pbk : alk. paper)
1. Philosophy — Introductions. 2. Skepticism. I. Title.
BD21.P44 1996   95–36644
100 — dc20   CIP

Typeset in 11 on 13pt Bembo
by CentraCet Limited, Cambridge

Printed and bound in Great Britain by
Marston Lindsay Ross International Ltd,
Oxfordshire

Contents

Analytical Table
of Contents

1. Philosophers' Doubts

What is philosophy about? (1); – Philosopher as ultra-cautious (1); – What the philosopher is prepared to doubt (2–3); – Examples to show why the senses cannot give us knowledge and objections to them (3–5); – Philosophical doubt not practical doubt (5); – Philosophical doubt as neurotic doubt (5–6); – Philosophical doubt as pseudo-doubt (6–7); – The route to deep scepticism about the possibility of knowledge and certainty in sense-experience (7–8); – knowledge and belief (8–9); – necessary truths and contingent truths (9–11); – certainty and empirical propositions (11–14).

2. Minds and the External World

Sense experiences and the external world: the sceptical challenge (15–16); – perception, imagination and memory (16–18); – sense data (18–19); – immediate experience and external circumstances (19–21); – imagination and memory (21–4).

3. Primary and Secondary Qualities

Reasons for distinguishing between primary and secondary qualities (25–6); – Are secondary qualities 'in the mind'? (26–9); – Secondary qualities as dispositional, relational and mental (29–31); – sceptical challenges concerning the identity of secondary qualities (31–3); –

9. Political Obligation

10. Aesthetic Values

11. Believing in God

12. Behaviour, Explanation and Criticism

13. Interrupting the Conversations of Mankind

Preface

In writing this introduction to philosophy, I have taken no prior knowledge of philosophy for granted in the reader. My aim has been to introduce readers to central issues in philosophy without simplifying them. So although I have written for those who are coming to philosophy for the first time, I hope that others will find what I have said to be of interest.

Despite introducing issues from widely different areas of philosophy, I have endeavoured to make my argument a continuous one. There is a fundamental theme which runs through the essay: the challenge of scepticism. Scepticism, at its deepest, challenges the very possibility of sense. There may be arguments over whether a particular claim to know something is sound, arguments over the colour of an object, or arguments over whether or not a figure we see is a human being. But deep scepticism asks whether it makes sense to say that we can know any empirical fact, whether it makes sense to speak of the colour of anything, and whether one can ever be sure that other human beings exist. There may be arguments over moral, political or aesthetic matters, but deep scepticism asks whether there is anything to argue over. Does it make sense to speak of moral and political obligation, or of aesthetic values? People argue about the reality of God. Deep scepticism questions the very possibility of religious sense.

Scepticism is often occasioned by serious differences and distances between human beings. Some philosophers have argued that its challenge can only be met by showing that these differences and distances are only apparent, not real. I argue in this essay that the challenge can be met without denying them. To deny the differences and distances is to deny our common experience.

Like anyone writing an introduction, I was faced with the issue of how it should be presented. It may be thought that writing an introduction to philosophy should be easy. It certainly is not. From the outset, I was determined to present an argument rather than a survey. Many surveys take the form of presenting different points of view, and then letting the readers make up their own minds. My determination not to do so was informed by a remark by one of my former teachers about such enterprises: 'How can you teach anyone to think unless they see you thinking?'

My material, in the main, has been taken from lecture courses that I have written over the years on Plato; the British empiricists, Locke, Berkeley and Hume; on scepticism; on metaphilosophy, a course based on Stanley Cavell's *The Claim of Reason*; on utilitarianism, Bentham and Mill; on Kant's moral philosophy; on twentieth-century ethics; on political philosophy – Hobbes, Locke, Rousseau and Hume; on Freud; and on the philosophy of religion. I have also made use of my published work in ethics and the philosophy of religion. In the lectures and published work I have, of course, discussed the work of many philosophers, agreeing and disagreeing with them, borrowing arguments and examples from others whenever I thought it beneficial. I have done the same in this essay. Acknowledgements are made in the notes at the end of the volume, since I did not want to interrupt the argument by citing authors. This had been my mistake in previous attempts at writing an introduction. By getting involved in detailed expositions, readings and counter-readings, criticisms and counter-criticisms, I ended up not seeing the wood for the trees. I became involved in a critical commentary instead of writing the kind of introduction to philosophy that I wanted. I have therefore presented a continuous argument without mentioning any philosophers by name. The loss in doing so is any sense of a historical development of the problems. The gain, hopefully, is to engage my readers in discussion.

I hope that readers will be helped by the analytical table of
contents that I have provided. Of course, it has not been possible
to cover every topic. Readers may be disappointed that certain
issues are not raised, or that objections which occur to them are
not considered. They may also regard certain arguments as
unsatisfactory. They may also agree with some of the conclusions
reached, but want to take them further. In the event of any of
these reactions, the introduction will have served its purpose in
prompting readers to go on reflective journeys of their own.

D. Z. Phillips

Acknowledgements

I gratefully acknowledge the sabbatical leave given to me by the University College of Swansea during the Michaelmas Term of 1992, during which I wrote the first version of this introduction. I am grateful to Melissa Norton for reading this essay and for the comments she made on it; to Helen Baldwin for preparing the typescript; and to Timothy Tessin for help with the proof-reading. Membership of a department which remained small for many years afforded me the opportunity of teaching a wide variety of courses. Without that opportunity, it would have been impossible to contemplate writing this introduction.

D.Z.P.

1

Philosophers' Doubts

What is philosophy about? Before I went to university, but knowing that philosophy was going to be one of the subjects I was to study there, I read a well-known introduction to philosophy in the hope of answering that question. My first impression was that the philosopher is an ultra-cautious person. Philosophers do not rush into saying that we know this or that, as most people do. They step back and think about things. Although we say we know all sorts of things, strictly speaking – philosophers conclude – we do not.

Given this view of philosophy, it seemed to me that the usefulness of philosophy was evident. Philosophy is a way of sharpening our thinking. It teaches us to be cautious, and not to be over-hasty in reaching our conclusions. By imposing its strict demands philosophy tightens up our standards of knowledge. Our day-to-day assumptions are shot through with contradictions and inconsistencies. A great deal of reflection is necessary before we can arrive at what we really know. Philosophy is an indispensable guide in this reflection. This view of the usefulness of philosophy was reflected in the views of many educationalists, and this is still the case. They favour introductory classes in philosophy even for those whose primary intentions are to study other subjects. The pencil needs to be sharpened before it can write with sufficient care about other topics.

This straightforward view of philosophy was given a severe jolt,

however, when I read further and discovered the kinds of thing
that many philosophers were prepared to doubt.[1] They doub
things that we ordinarily would not doubt. The list that I read ir
the introduction to philosophy was surprising, to say the least. The
philosopher told me that it seemed to him, at a certain moment
that he was sitting in a chair at a table which had a certain shape
on which he saw sheets of paper with writing or print on them
By turning his head he could see buildings, clouds and the sur
through the window. He believed that the sun is about ninety-
three million miles away from the Earth and that, owing to the
Earth's rotation, it rises every morning and will continue to do so
for an indefinite time in the future. He believed that if any other
normal person came into the room, that person would see the
same chairs, tables, books and papers as he saw. Further, he
believed that the table he saw was the same table as he felt pressing
against his arm.

What puzzled me was this: on the one hand, the philosopher
wrote that all these things seemed so evident as to be hardly worth
stating; but on the other hand, he said that all these facts could be
reasonably doubted and that much reflection is needed before we
can arrive at a description of the situation which would be wholly
true. Of course, he was quite prepared to admit that most people
would not bother to question these facts. They would see no
point in doing so. My initial reaction was to think that the
majority were correct on this issue. Suddenly, in view of what the
philosopher was prepared to doubt, philosophy, so far from
appearing to be a useful subject, now appeared to be a complete
waste of time. The philosophical doubt seemed to be, not a
tightening up of standards, but a trivial game; the kind of game
which irritates parents when, on the first visit home after comm-
encing the subject, budding philosophers confront them with the
question, 'So you think there's a table here, do you?' Recently,
some philosophers have reacted in the same way to philosophers'
doubts. They have asked why philosophers should give young
people doubts that they would never have had in the first place if
the philosophers had not opened their mouths. On this view,
philosophy does not clarify our confusions – it creates them.[2]

My new reaction, however, simply led to a new puzzle. Why should we doubt what seems so evident as to not need stating? Surely, it is not enough simply to accuse philosophers of indulging in trivial pursuits. They take their doubts seriously. I felt there was something wrong about these doubts, but did not know why. Whether we like it or not, people have always been puzzled about the doubts that philosophers discuss. I felt it was insufficient to say to someone who has doubts about whether we *know* something, 'Well, we *do*, so that's that'. Even if we feel that there is something odd about the philosophical doubts, that response will not help the doubter. The doubter is not going to accept the answer on authority. If the doubt is misplaced, we have to show the route by which it is reached. Unless we show the road to confusion, there is no road back from it.

But what is the road to philosophical doubt? There is no one answer to that question. I was introduced to the challenge of philosophical scepticism through one of the oldest philosophical questions about the search for knowledge: Should we regard our senses as a reliable guide in the search? It does not seem that we should, since the senses often mislead us. What confidence can we have, therefore, that we are not also being misled on the other occasions on which we trust them? Think of examples of situations which may mislead us: a stick partly immersed in water appears to be bent; we are deceived by what we think we see in a fog; a house's appearance differs depending on the position from which we look at it; colours change under different light conditions; something which tastes sweet to one person may taste bitter to another; water feels hot to one hand and cold to another; and so on.

But, then, when we begin to think about them, we may wonder why examples such as these should lead us to conclude that the senses cannot be trusted. There are three reasons for this reaction. First, in describing the examples, we seem to trust the senses well enough. Even if we are misled by the apparent shape of the stick, what about the stick itself, the water and the glass? We do not doubt these in describing the example. A house's appearance may vary from different perspectives, but the existence of the house is taken for granted. The existence of the substance which tastes differently to different people is not questioned; nor is the existence of objects the colours of which vary under different light conditions. We speak unhesitatingly of the water which feels both hot and cold. So the examples take empirical facts for granted while purporting to show that such reliance is unjustified.

Second, it seems that such examples move illegitimately from *particular* cases of deception to *general* sceptical conclusions concerning the senses. After all, as other philosophers have pointed out, once we have had the phenomenon explained to us, we *expect* a stick partly immersed in water to look bent. A philosopher once took a stick partly immersed in water into a lecture. When the stick was taken out of the water, it turned out to be a bent stick. Wouldn't we be amazed if we saw everything clearly in a fog? What would we make of a chair which looked the same no matter from what position it is viewed? What if we walked three miles to a hilltop, looked down at our house, and found that it looked as it does when we are standing six feet away from it? Our sense of perspective involves different expectations about how the house will look. Do we not expect colours to be affected by different light conditions? Aren't tastes, touches and smells affected by changing circumstances? These examples are supposed to lead to a general scepticism about the senses, but it appears that they seldom mislead us even in particular cases.[3]

Third, in these examples, we do not pay enough attention to the fact that the circumstances invoked are *unfavourable*. It is these unfavourable circumstances which give our doubts their foothold and plausibility: the stick was partly immersed in water, we were trying to see in a fog, light conditions kept changing, and so on. Our doubts were practical doubts. When we remove the unfavourable circumstances, our doubts are removed at the same time. Our doubts lift with the fog. We can take practical measures to allay our doubts, so why should they lead to general scepticism about the senses?

So far, I have outlined three initial reactions to philosophical doubt. First, the examples said to cause the doubt rely on the very empirical facts which we are supposed not to be able to rely on.

Second, so far from misleading us, the examples illustrate what has become part of our normal expectations in various circumstances. Third, the examples rely on unfavourable circumstances which we can come to terms with. Why, then, should such examples lead anyone, including philosophers, to conclude that the senses cannot give us knowledge?

Once I began studying philosophy, I soon became dissatisfied with these initial reactions. This was because they neglected what, in many ways, seems at first to be the oddest feature of these philosophical doubts. The philosophers doubt what, ordinarily, we would not dream of questioning. Can we treat the philosophical doubts as though they are straightforward practical doubts? Clearly, they are not. The doubts seem to be entertained in the absence of any practical reason for doing so. Suppose I am doubtful, while driving in a fog, whether there is a tree looming up before me. I may slow down, get out of the car, walk up to the tree, even touch it. I confirm that the tree is there. I settle my practical doubt. But we are not always driving on foggy days. We sometimes drive on clear days. We look at trees, we may sit in their branches, pick fruit from them, chop them down, and so on. We have no practical doubt about the trees. There is nothing to confirm. But, even in these *ideal* circumstances, some philosophers continue to doubt.

What can this doubt amount to? In the previous examples, our doubts made sense in the context of unfavourable circumstances which we could contrast with favourable circumstances in which we did not doubt. But when philosophers doubt what the senses yield in favourable circumstances, what contrast can be drawn to give this doubt any sense? Apparently none. It seems that we have nowhere to go.

Well, perhaps not nowhere. There *are* people who doubt even in favourable circumstances. We call them neurotics. I once lived opposite a man who went through the same routine every morning on his way to work. He had doubts over whether he had closed his front door properly. Having pulled it shut, he would rattle and turn the door handle vigorously for some seconds before pushing the door hard. He would then step back from the door before repeating the whole sequence of checks. He would then walk halfway down his garden path, before returning to the door to repeat the checks yet again. Finally, he would come out of his gate and walk halfway along the hedge, before rushing back to the front door to give its handle its last rattle. Certainly, the man had neurotic doubts. But neurotic doubts make philosophical doubt all the more puzzling.

A minority of philosophers have been attracted by the comparison between philosophical doubt and neurotic doubt. They have tried to trace philosophers' doubts to some aspect of their personal lives which would account for them. For example, a philosopher's reluctance to say that the senses can give us knowledge may be traced to an abhorrence of or disdain for the flesh, the legacy of a certain kind of Christianity. The trouble with suggestions such as these, however, is that they ignore or by-pass the *philosophical* character of the doubts that we are discussing.

We cannot simply accept the comparison between philosophical doubt and neurotic doubt uncritically. A neurosis shows itself in the behaviour of the person concerned. Were it not so there would be no point in calling it a neurosis. But philosophical doubt is not accompanied by these neurotic symptoms. So what does the philosophical doubt amount to if it is not accompanied by the kind of behaviour which gives practical and neurotic doubt their sense? If philosophical doubt does not make *that* kind of difference, what kind of difference *does* it make? If it makes *no* difference, what on Earth is the point of it?

Because of the apparent pointlessness of sceptical doubt, some philosophers have called it pseudo-doubt. Outside philosophy, this reaction can be found among those who show little patience with the subject, saying that they do not need philosophy to tell them whether there are tables or chairs in a room. But if *that* is what philosophers mean when they call sceptical doubt pseudo-doubt, why don't they give up the subject? After all, if we take away the issues which arise from philosophical doubt, how much of philosophy is left?

Some philosophers have replied to this question by saying that they remain within philosophy to point out to other philosophers that their sceptical doubts are misplaced. They speak as if philosophy is a form of bewitchment. But, then, even if there is bewitchment, what is the character of the battle against it? Isn't that battle philosophical? But how is the battle to be waged? Some have replied: by reminding the doubters of what we all know. We return them to common-sense. If a philosopher says that we cannot be certain of any empirical fact, we can simply reply, 'Of course we can. We are certain of hundreds of facts of that kind.' We simply tell these philosophers that we do not doubt on those occasions when the philosophers say we must.[4]

This reaction still does not answer the puzzle concerning the nature of philosophical doubt. In fact, it helps to increase the puzzle. The sceptical philosophers are accused of ignorance. All they need to deliver them from this ignorance, it seems, is a series of reminders. The difficulty with the suggestion, however, is that the doubting philosophers clearly know what they are supposed to be ignorant of. They know that most people speak of knowledge where they do not. They are fully aware that people say, for example, that they know that there are tables and chairs in a room. But that does not get them to give up their doubts. On the contrary, they would claim that philosophical reflection shows that we do not know the things we think we know.[5] Why should we accept common-sense or what we ordinarily say as our norm? They would argue that our standards of knowledge should be what we arrive at after philosophical reflection, standards which show that we *should* doubt our senses even when, ordinarily, we do not. Mere factual reminders to philosophers accuse them of confusion in their scepticism. But if confusion is present, such reminders do not reveal the route by which the confusion comes about. The reminders leave out the philosophy.

To appreciate the nature of philosophical doubt about the senses at its deepest, we must see that what is being denied is *the possibility* of knowledge where the senses are concerned. Why is this possibility denied? Philosophers are rightly impressed by an important distinction between knowledge and belief. I may have good reason for saying that I know that there is a chair in the next room. I may have put it there a few minutes ago. Yet, unknown to me, in that brief interval, someone has removed it. On finding this out, I can say that I *thought* I knew the chair was in the room, but I cannot say that I *knew* it was there. On the other hand, if I said that I believed the chair was in the next room, and this turned out to be false, I can still say that I believed it. But I have to retract my claim to knowledge. What I know must be so, whereas what I claim to know need not be so.

From these correct observations, however, some philosophers take a further unjustifiable step. Instead of saying that what I know must be so, they say that what I know *must always be so.*[6] Only that which *could not turn out to be* false deserves to be called knowledge. But, it is said, any empirical proposition *could* turn out to be false. Therefore it follows that no empirical proposition can ever amount to knowledge. If we want to appreciate what the sceptic is saying about the senses, we should not say that we can never know or be certain that there is a chair in the room, that a table is red, or that lemons are bitter. If we put the matter in this way, it looks as if these propositions fall short of a standard that they *ought* to attain. It looks as though they are failing a test. But that is misleading. What the sceptic is saying is that the standard which knowledge needs simply does not apply to empirical propositions. They do not fail the test of knowledge, since the test simply does not apply to them. 'Knowledge' and 'certainty' are simply not appropriate where empirical propositions are concerned.[7]

If, as we have seen, knowledge is to be restricted to propositions which *cannot* turn out to be false, where can such propositions be found? The answer is: in logic and mathematics. Consider the law of identity in logic, which may be expressed as 'A is A'. If we try to contradict the proposition, we end up with nonsense. We cannot say 'A is not A'. The same conclusions can be drawn with the propositions of mathematics, such as '2 + 2 = 4'. We cannot say '2 + 2 = 5'. It has no application in mathematics. We are told that the interior angles of a triangle equal two right angles. If someone said, 'I think that's too hasty. We should wait to see if a triangle turns up to which this does not apply', that would show a failure to grasp the meaning of 'triangle'. Another way of putting the matter is to say that a necessary truth is being treated as though it were a contingent truth. When the sceptic says that we can never be certain about any empirical proposition, what is being said is that only necessary propositions give us knowledge.

It has seemed to some philosophers that in the propositions of logic and mathematics we have a certainty which cannot be found in any empirical proposition. But wherein does the necessity of '2 + 2 = 4' reside? It is tempting to say that the necessary truth of the proposition derives from the signs employed in it. But this is misleading. Suppose that beings on another planet found a piece of paper among the remains of a failed space mission. On it is written '2 + 2 = 4'. They are impressed by these marks. They decorate surfaces with them, and so the marks have an application among them. We are not tempted to say that this application contradicts our mathematics. How could design patterns do that? But what if the beings on the other planet have an alternative mathematics, one in which '2 + 2 = 5' is correct? Are we not tempted to say that this mathematics contradicts ours? Are we not tempted to say that the beings on the other planet *cannot* say '2 + 2 = 5' because the meanings of the terms '2', '5', '+' and '=' make that impossible? But what are the meanings of these terms? How do we find this out? Surely by looking at the role they play in our mathematics and its application. In other words, it is not the terms which generate the arithmetic, but the arithmetic which gives meaning to the terms. Therefore the alternative mathematics does not contradict ours. Given the place of '2 + 2 = 5' in our mathematics, its contradictory is ruled out as nonsense.[8]

Philosophers then point out that, in contrast to the necessary truths of logic and mathematics, the contradictory of an empirical proposition always makes sense. Empirical propositions are called contingent because their truth or falsity depends on changing circumstances. Where physical objects are concerned, it is insufficient to speak of their extension, something they share with geometrical objects. We have also to speak of their solidity. To find out truths about the empirical world, reflection is not enough. We have to look, observe and experiment. What we find out depends on circumstances. If we said that the interior angles of a triangle did not equal two right angles, that would involve a change in our conception of a triangle. But if the proposition 'It is raining' is true one day, and the proposition 'It is not raining' is true the next day, there has been no change in the meaning of 'It is raining'. What has changed is the circumstances. From day to day we have to look to see what is the case. For this reason, it is argued, what we find out are contingent, not necessary, truths. And contingent truths, it is said, cannot be called knowledge.

What we see emerging in the argument is the idea of two realms. In one realm, we have necessary truths which give us knowledge. In the other realm, we have contingent truths which do not deserve the name 'knowledge'. They yield only opinion. The propositions of logic and mathematics give us knowledge, whereas empirical propositions only give us opinion. As we have seen, there are important differences between these different propositions, but should these lead us to talk of 'knowledge' in the one case and of 'opinion' in the other?

What is it that tempts us to draw this distinction, apart from the considerations we have already mentioned? In the case of logic and mathematics we can see why a given conclusion or answer *must* be arrived at. We are presented with the rationale which shows us what must necessarily be so. Our questions come to an end when the logic of this necessity is made manifest to us. By comparison, the end of our enquiries where the senses are concerned seems arbitrary by comparison. For example, why should we call anything *the* colour of an object? In asking that question, we are not doubting the colour of a particular object as we would be doing were our doubt a practical one. If we wonder whether an object is red or green, we are not questioning the reality of colours. On the contrary, our query takes that reality for granted. But have we any right to do that? We may say that a table is brown. But, as we all know, parts of it are brighter or darker than others. Some parts do not look brown at all. We know that its colour will change in different light conditions. So why speak about *the* colour of the table? We may be told that by *the* colour is meant how the table looks in certain light conditions to people with normal eyesight. But why pick on how the table looks to certain people in certain conditions and grant it the status of knowledge? It has none of the necessity of the rationale provided by the examples of necessary truths in logic and mathematics. What we call *the* colour seems a matter of arbitrary choice and opinion.

What is more, it seems that there is no way out from the realm of opinion for the senses. I may look at two lines and think they are equal when they are unequal. Here we have a distinction between how the lines *seem* and how the lines *are*. What enables us to make the distinction is measurement. We are no longer dependent on appearances. Measurement enables us to arrive at the real truth concerning the lines. But, it may be asked, can't we do the same where the senses are concerned? Here, too, we can distinguish between how things are and how things seem. There may seem to be a tall tree in a fog, but when the fog lifts we find out that there is not. In certain light conditions an object may seem to be of a certain colour, but in daylight we come to see what its real colour is. But these contrasts in the realm of the senses may not satisfy us. When we contrasted how the lines looked with how they are, we were able to turn from appearances to measurement. In the case of colours this is not so. In our example, we contrast how the table looks in special light conditions with how it looks in daylight. But all we do, it seems, is to pass from one 'look' to another. We cannot escape from the world of appearances. Why give one appearance precedence over the other? Is not the matter purely arbitrary?

But what does this use of 'arbitrary' amount to? Do we mean 'arbitrary' when compared with the necessity of conclusions and answers in logic and mathematics? But this makes it look as if we are subjecting the two categories of propositions to a common test, with empirical propositions proving to be inferior to the others. But this cannot be right, since, as we have seen, the philosophers who deny that the senses can give us knowledge say that such a comparison is misleading. Empirical propositions do not fail any test. It is simply that 'knowledge' and 'certainty' do not belong to propositions of this kind. But what this amounts to is setting up one kind of discourse, the propositions of logic and mathematics, as a *paradigm* of knowledge. Anything which does not answer to the paradigm is simply refused that status. This is highly misleading, since it obscures from us the ways in which we do speak of knowledge and certainty where the senses are concerned.

Consider again the example in which I say I know that there are chairs in a room. When challenged, I say that my reason for saying so is that I put them there a few minutes ago. This is a perfectly good reason for my claim to knowledge. What would override it would be, for example, the fact that the chairs have been removed by someone since I had put them there. This is the kind of thing which threatens my claim to knowledge. But this is not what the sceptical philosopher offers me. I am told that 'There are chairs in the room' can never constitute knowledge because its contradictory, unlike the contradictory of '2 + 2 = 4', *always* makes sense. But what bearing does the possibility of my framing the contradictory of 'There are chairs in the room', in the abstract, have on whether I say that there are chairs in the room? None whatsoever. It has no bearing on the issue.

The same is true where certainty is concerned. If I walk into a lecture room full of students, I can, at the same time, construct the contradictory of the proposition, 'There are students in the lecture room'. But this abstract possibility would have no bearing on my certainty. This example is an interesting one, because some philosophers say that whereas the contradictory of the propositions of logic and mathematics never make sense, the contradictory of an empirical proposition always makes sense. But is this true? Is it true no matter what the circumstances?[9] Consider the circumstances in which I am lecturing to a large class. I may make a mistake about the exact number of students in the class. I may say there are two hundred present when in fact there are two hundred and thirty there. I may make a mistake in thinking a particular student is present when that is not the case. These are mistakes that I may make. But what if someone suggested that as I taught there were no students in the class? What could I make of that suggestion? If I am not certain that I am lecturing to a room full of students, what can I be certain of? If I mistake the number of students, I can count them. If I do not know whether someone is present, I can ask the student to stand up. But if I am told as I lecture to a room full of students that I may be mistaken, apart from dismissing the suggestion as a joke, what else can I do? I cannot turn to appeal to a better situation, since I am already in the kind of situation I would appeal to if my circumstances were unfavourable. I may wonder whether a lecture room has students in it, so I look inside to find out. But in the example we are considering, I am already lecturing to the students. So here are circumstances where, for me, and for anyone else in the lecture, the proposition 'There are no students in this room' has no application, no sense. We cannot say that the proposition could be true, but happens to be false, as we could say of a proposition concerning the number of students in the lecture. The truth of the proposition has no application to give it sense.

I am not saying that it could not turn out that there were no students in the lecture room. What would I have to imagine? Suppose that a porter, with a concerned look on his face, interrupts after I have been lecturing for about fifteen minutes. He says, 'I am sorry to interrupt you, but this room is empty'. You must imagine this actually happening to you. Do not speculate about it in the abstract. Suppose that he and others actually convince me that the room is empty. What then? Do I go home and say, 'I made a rather big mistake today. I thought I was lecturing to two hundred students when in fact the room was empty'? Of course not. I would be terrified! I would think I was going mad! It would be absurd to compare this situation with one in which I have to decide whether or not there are students in a lecture room. In the situation that I am envisaging, I would not know any more what it would mean to take such discussions one way or the other. This is shown by the fact that, in such a state, what I would need is not correction, but treatment.

This does not mean that the sense in which '2 + 2 = 4' cannot be contradicted is the same as the sense in which we could not contemplate the contradictory of the proposition 'There are students in this room' in a lecture room full of students. But it does show how misleading it is to impose a paradigm for certainty, based on propositions of one kind, on propositions of quite a different kind. The differences between the propositions should not lead us to say that knowledge and certainty can only be found in the propositions of logic and mathematics. What we need to see is what 'knowledge' and 'certainty' come to in this context, and also in our talk of empirical matters. In doing so, we can be brought to see, at the same time, why philosophers have been led to deny *the possibility* of knowledge and certainty in the realm of the senses.

2

Minds and the External World

We have seen why it has been said that the senses can give us opinion, but not knowledge. We started by considering examples such as thinking that we see a tree in a fog, or thinking that an object has a certain colour in special light conditions. In these examples we simply took the existence of an external world for granted, but do we have any right to do so? If we come to know many things by means of our senses, do not these things include the external world? If so, do we not have to face the following sceptical challenge: If I know through my senses, what reason have I for thinking that I am in contact with an external world?

How do I come to know anything? Before I know anything my mind must have been like an empty receptacle, waiting to receive knowledge. Where is this knowledge to come from? Surely, from something outside myself, something which will furnish my mind with knowledge. How else am I to become acquainted with 'yellow', 'red', 'hardness', 'softness', 'hot', 'cold', 'sweetness', 'bitterness', and so on? These are experiences that I receive as a result of my interaction with the external world. I call the experiences that I have 'ideas', 'impressions' or 'sensations'. These are the furnishings of my mind, the data on which any knowledge I have relies.

But, now, a sceptical worry surfaces. If the sensory experiences of my mind are my necessary starting-point in my search for knowledge, how do I ever get beyond them? I say that these experiences come from an external world, but how do I know this? If my mind is acquainted only with its own ideas, how do I know – how can I know – whether these ideas refer to anything? How can I know that they refer to an external world? The very *possibility* of knowledge of an external world seems thrown into question.

Consider 'seeing' as an example; seeing a table, let us say. I want to say that this experience came about as a result of something external to itself, namely, the table. But how can I ever know that? How do I get from my experience, my idea of the table, to the real table? If I have an experience called 'seeing a table' I have an obvious interest in knowing whether it refers to a table. My experience may have been caused by some other object, or by no object at all. Light conditions may create the illusion that I am seeing a table. But how can I find out whether my experience does refer to a table, or to some other object, or whether it is illusory? If I want to know what causes the bulge in my sock, I can take out the object causing the bulge, a golf ball, let us say, and find out by doing so. In this example I have an independent access to the cause of the bulge in my sock. But when I want to know the cause of the ideas in my mind, I can have no independent access to their cause. But in that case, how do I know that they are caused by anything or refer to anything? I seem to be locked in the circle of my own ideas.

Let us suppose that my mental experience takes the form of an image of an apple. How can I know whether I am seeing an apple or imagining an apple? If I am imagining an apple, my experience makes no contact with a real apple. But, once again, I can only check this if I have independent access to the apple, the very access which seems to be denied to me. How on Earth am I going to get out of this predicament? There seems to be only one direction in which to look for an answer. If my mind is acquainted only with its own ideas, there must be something *about the ideas themselves* which tells me which refer to an external reality and which do not. If this were so, the hold of the sceptical challenge would be broken.

Is it not the case that the ideas connected with perception, with 'seeing an apple', are more consistent than ideas connected with imagination, with 'imagining an apple'? I shall be able to tell, therefore, from the consistency of my ideas, whether they refer to an apple. But there is an obvious objection to this suggestion. No matter how consistent a pattern my ideas may have, this pattern is quite consistent with the non-existence of the apple. Consistency in my ideas cannot guarantee the existence of the apple. I seem no further ahead in my predicament.

Why is the appeal to the qualitative character of my experiences so appealing? It trades on examples in which the qualitative character of our experiences is important in deciding what we are hearing or seeing. The sounds we hear may be distinct or indistinct. In the latter case we may say, 'I think I hear the bus coming, but I can't be sure', whereas in the former I may say without hesitation, 'Here comes the bus'. I may say, 'I think there's a house in the distance where we can go for help, but it's hard to see clearly in this fog' – and so on. But, once again, it is essential to note that we have *independent* checks on what I claim to hear or see. The bus arrives or fails to arrive. We arrive or fail to arrive at the house. Neither am I dependent solely on myself in such checks. The checks include what other people say. I may say, 'I saw the ferry set out last night', only to be told, 'You can't have. We were repairing it in dock at the time'. But in the appeal which is restricted to the quality of ideas in the mind, these independent checks are ruled out. The problem then is to show how it is possible, on such a basis, to distinguish between perception and imagination.

Let us consider another suggestion. Can't we tell from our mental experiences whether we are imagining something or remembering something, because memory ideas are far livelier?[1] But the same objections return. No matter how lively my idea of a harbour may be, this is still compatible with it not being a memory of an actual harbour. Furthermore, it does not seem plausible to suggest that my haziest recollections will be livelier than my most vivid imaginings. It could be argued, however, that it could still be said, despite these conceptions, that memories are livelier than imaginings. After all, although a given quantity of cork may be heavier than a different quantity of lead, we can still say generally that lead is heavier than cork. But for reasons with which we are familiar by now, this analogy does not save us from the sceptical challenge. We can say that lead is heavier than cork because, independent of both, we have a system of measurement which allows us to reach this conclusion. But we are asked to say from ideas in the mind alone, and in the absence of any external check, whether these experiences are perceptions, imaginings or memories.

Another suggestion fares equally badly. We may think that our ideas come with 'indicators' which tell us their identity. Again, we may think of occasions when thinking of one aspect of a situation helps us to remember another. But whether we are remembering correctly depends on an independent check, something other than the memory claim. Furthermore, if our ideas in the mind came equipped with indicators which somehow informed us, 'This is a perception', 'This is a memory' or 'This is an imagining', why should we ever make mistakes? And is not that part of the sceptical worry? We think that we are seeing or remembering when we are merely imagining. What if all our ideas are idle imaginings, having no reference to an external world? And if I am locked in the circle of my own ideas how can I ever know that that is not the case?

I do not seem to be getting very far in answering the sceptical challenge, but is this because the challenge has been accepted on its own terms? Perhaps we ought to question the initial starting-point of the challenge, the assumption that all I am acquainted with are the ideas of my own mind. What is it that makes this assumption attractive? Think of examples such as hearing a car in the distance. It may be said that to say I hear a car is to say more than I know, strictly speaking. I am going beyond the immediate datum of my experience. That immediate datum is a sound. That is what I can be said to know. In saying that it is the sound of a car, I am interpreting the sound, perhaps by association with other occasions, and so on.

For examples such as these, the illegitimate assumption is made that *all* our experiences are based on minimal, immediate data.

Thus, although there is nothing wrong in saying that I see a book, I am told that this is a very complex claim. What I experience immediately, it is said, is not a book, but a certain diversity of light and colour. These immediate data are self-authenticating. We cannot be mistaken about them. They are called *sense-data*. When we say that we see tables and chairs we are clearly going beyond our immediate experience of sense-data. The sceptical challenge can now be reformulated in these terms: What is the relation between our experience of sense-data and our claim to experience an external world? How can we ever get from sense-data to knowledge of the external world? Claims about the external world always stand in need of evidence. Sense-data, on the other hand, provide the evidence. But the problem is that sense-data can never provide sufficient justification for saying that we are in contact with an external world. Let us see why.[2]

What qualifies as an example of an indubitable immediate experience? 'I hear a car' clearly does not qualify, since that is a claim that I could be mistaken about. But 'I hear a purring engine-like noise' will not qualify either, since I could be mistaken about that too. I may have forgotten that I have cotton-wool in my ears, and the noise may, in fact, be quite a loud one. Will 'I hear a noise' qualify as a minimal, immediate experience? No, because I may be mistaken about that too. What I am hearing is simply noises in my head. And so we arrive at a minimal sense-datum: 'It seems to me now as if I were hearing a noise.'

The outcome of our quest for an example of a minimal sense-experience is not encouraging. We must not forget that the purpose of locating such data was to provide evidence for claims concerning the external world. We were supposed to be enabled to *advance* from such data to statements concerning the external world. But the location of such data constitutes, not an advance to, but a retreat from any claims about the external world. In terms of our example, the retreat takes the following form: 'I hear a car' – 'I seem to hear a car' – 'It seems to *me* I hear a car' – 'It seems to me *now* that I hear a purring-noise' – 'It seems to me now as though I were hearing a purring-noise'.

Why did we go in search of minimal sense-data in the first

place? We did so because we felt that any statement about an external world can always be doubted, and thus stands in need of evidence. What we know immediately are minimal sense-data. But is this true? As we saw in the last chapter, we doubt in circumstances that we call unfavourable. But what of favourable circumstances? Can I doubt that I hear a car in these? The car may be coming directly towards me. I may be sitting in the car or driving it. There may be no room for doubt at all. It would be absurd to suggest that there is always room for doubt because I may have forgotten that I had cotton-wool in my ears. It would be odd to say that any kind of judgement or verdict on the basis of sense-data is necessary when, in favourable circumstances, we hear a car. Verdicts are needed, for the most part, when we are not in a position to hear or see things clearly. But if I am sitting at a table, leaning on it, and so on, I am not giving a verdict on anything. My sitting at a table is not a claim which stands in need of evidence. It is not a claim at all. When I see a book, select it, pick it up, turn its pages and read it, I am not verifying anything. I am simply seeing, selecting, picking up, turning the pages and reading a book.

Whether a statement stands in need of evidence depends on the circumstances in which it is made. Once this is admitted, we can see that there is no absolute distinction between two kinds of statement — one kind of statement which always stands in need of evidence, and another kind of statement which always provides evidence. So we cannot say that any statement about the external world stands in need of evidence and that it is the function of statements about sense-data to provide such evidence. But once this absolute distinction is rejected, we reject the terms of the sceptical challenge at the same time. It can no longer be said that we *must* show how knowledge of an external world can be arrived at on the basis of the immediate data of our experience. Indeed, when circumstances are favourable, the onus is not on us to say when we can stop doubting and be able to assert 'I see a book'. The onus is on the sceptic to tell us why we should have started to doubt in the first place.

Once we appreciate the importance of circumstances in seeing when it does or does not makes sense to ask for evidence for statements, we see that they are equally central in determining conditions of intelligibility. As a result, we can ask whether the dichotomy involved in the sceptical challenge makes sense. We are told that we have to start from the mind and its experiences, and show how, on such a basis, we can be justified in talking of an external world. But is the notion of this inner world of mental experiences cut off from anything external to it an intelligible one?[3]

As we saw in the last chapter, we are sometimes mistaken about what we think we perceive. I see a stick partly immersed in water and think it is bent. Later I find out that I was mistaken. The stick was not bent. But what I saw was bent. What, then, did I see? It is tempting to reply, 'Not the stick, but the appearance of the stick'. What 'appears', the sense-datum, does not guarantee any reference to what is really the case. By such an argument, experiences become a 'something' between me and objects in the external world. In the case of illusions the 'something' that I experience does not refer to anything, whereas in the case of perceptions it does.

But this conception of a sense-datum, the necessary object of my experience, is a confused one. If I think I see a bent stick which later turns out to be straight, I do not need to postulate anything other than the stick to account for my mistake. I do not see 'the appearance' of the stick. It is the stick that looks bent. It is the *same* thing, namely, the stick, which – in certain conditions – appears to be bent when it is not. The phenomenon of deception does not necessitate the postulation of two realms, one of sense-data and the other of physical objects. That being so, we are not faced with the task of showing how we move from the first realm to the second.

Once we accept this conclusion, we can see why we are not faced with the task of justifying calling the various sense-data that we are said to experience, perceptions, memories or imaginings. We have already seen that we cannot resolve the matter by appealing to qualitative differences in the sense-data. And yet, according to the sceptic, we can appeal only to the data of our mental experiences. But this is where the sceptic relies on ignoring the circumstances in which our notions of perception, memory and imagination have their application. Consider, for example, the radical challenge to show how we can ever know that we are remembering anything. Memories have to do with the past, but since the past can never be recalled, it is said, how can what we call memories ever be checked? The challenge affects the most ordinary circumstances. If I see an apple, once the perception is over, it becomes a memory. But if the past cannot be recalled, how do I ever know that I am seeing the same apple as I saw on a previous occasion? How do I know I am looking at the same apple I looked at a minute ago?

We face this challenge only if we forget the circumstances in which we speak of our memories. The assumption that our memories can never be checked is false. If my memory tells me that a certain building has such-and-such an appearance, and is to be located at such-and-such a place, I may relocate that building and find that my memories are correct. The logical priority is the exact opposite of what the sceptic would have us believe. We are invited to start with sense-data called 'memories' and justify how we can know that they refer to anything real. But it is external circumstances which determine whether an 'experience' can be called a memory. We cannot remember that which has never taken place. And, of course, we check what has happened in various ways. We ask people, check records, revisit places, and so on. If the checks do not bear out what I say, I have to give up my claim to have remembered such-and-such. We also forget the limitations of time and place on what I can be said to remember. I cannot say that I remember sailing with Columbus, or seeing one of the goals which clinched Morriston Town Soccer Club's promotion to the First Division. But I can remember reading about Columbus and travelling to Preston to support Swansea and seeing the goals scored which secured that result.

If someone asks me how I know that someone is in a certain hotel, I may appeal to the fact that I remember seeing the person arrive. Of course, there are plenty of occasions on which my memory fails me. But this is something I also find out by checking in the ways I have described, not by appealing to the qualities of sense-data. It is in the context of such checks that our talk of people having good memories, bad memories, unreliable memories and fantastic memories has its sense. If we sever the connections between our memory claims and the surroundings that we have described, talk of memory itself becomes senseless. If memories were determined by the qualities of sense-data, to have such data would be to have memories, even if the events in question never occurred! This is one example of the unintelligibility we fall into when we sever the connection between memory-claims and the normal surroundings of our lives.

The unintelligibility involved in the notions of two realms, one of sense-data, and the other of external objects, is a far-reaching one. It may seem as if, irrespective of what we say of the latter, sense can be made of the notion of the mind and its sensory-experiences. After all, according to the sceptic, this is our necessary starting-point in our search for knowledge. But, logically, this is not the case. If we sever the connection between the notion of experience and our normal surroundings, the notion of the mind and its experiences will itself become unintelligible.

Consider the simple instruction, 'Think of a harbour'. I cannot obey it unless I know something about harbours. I must be able to recognize a harbour. Unless I can do this, someone will retort when I describe what I am thinking, 'No, that's not a harbour. You're thinking of something else'. My thinking, my mental image of a harbour, is not self-authenticating. It is by reference to harbours and our dealings with them that the correctness of my thinking will be assessed. I can obey the instructions, 'Think of a triangle', or 'Think of the colour "red"', only because I have a wider acquaintance with triangles and colours. But the sceptic thinks that we can strip away these wider surroundings and still speak intelligibly of the mind and its ideas. To him, the mind, so conceived, is unproblematic. What is problematic, it is claimed, is how we can ever know that we are in contact with the external world. The reverse is true. If we forget our external surroundings, the notion of the mind and its ideas becomes a meaningless concatenation of sensory data. The intelligibility of private experiences depends on external surroundings that we share.

It is important to realize that in considering counter-examples in combating the sceptics, we are not piling up counter-evidence in an attempt to convince them. We are not trying to verify our perceptions and memories. That would be a misunderstanding, as we shall see in greater detail in chapter 6. What we are doing, rather, is attempting to show the place that perceptions, memories and imagination occupy in our lives. Some features of these notions, as we have seen, may tempt us towards scepticism. But if we reflect on them carefully, we can come to see that that need not happen.

As we have seen, the sceptic tries to drive a wedge between the mind and its ideas on the one hand, and the external world on the other hand. We have examined the implications of doing so for our understanding of perception, memory and imagination. At the heart of the sceptical challenge is the notion of the mind of an individual as the passive recipient of experiences. That notion will be our concern in chapters 5 and 6.

3

Primary and Secondary Qualities

In the previous chapter, we discussed the sceptical challenge which sought to drive a wedge between the mind of the individual and the external world. If I am locked within my own ideas and experiences, dependent on the qualitative differences between them alone, how am I to know whether these ideas and experiences tell me anything about an external world? This is sometimes put by asking whether my experiences are subjective or objective.

We have argued against the terms of reference that the sceptic seeks to impose on us. According to the sceptic, our necessary starting-point in the search for knowledge is the mind of the individual and its ideas. This makes problematic how we are to arrive at a knowledge of the external world on that basis. We have argued that the reverse is the case. Without a reference to the shared surroundings of our lives, what becomes problematic is whether sense can be made of the mind and its ideas.

Yet, it may seem that that conclusion is too sweeping. May it not be the case that some of our experiences do indeed refer to how things are, but that others say more about ourselves than about any external reality? It need not be an all-or-nothing affair. May it not be that some of our experiences refer to an objective reality, while others are subjective? For example, do not our experiences of the shape, size and solidity of external objects refer to real qualities of those objects? For this reason they have been called the primary qualities of objects. But we also experience colours, tastes, smells and tactile sensations. Can we say that these experiences refer to what really is in the external world? Aren't we too involved in these experiences to say this? Some philosophers have certainly thought so. They have called the qualities concerned 'secondary qualities', and have claimed that they are not in the object, but in the mind.[1]

Consider the following example. A person places each of his hands into a bowl of water. To one hand the water feels hot, but, to the other hand the water feels cold. But *the same* water cannot be both hot and cold. We cease to be puzzled once we see that it doesn't make sense to ask *of the water* whether it is hot or cold. Felt heat or cold are to do with our reactions to the water, not with the water itself. Heat and cold are subjective human reactions. If fire warms us at a certain distance from it, but causes pain in us if we get too close, why should we attribute warmth to the fire when we would not dream of attributing pain to it?

If we want to know the real state of the water we must find out its temperature. This is not subject to our subjective fluctuations, and has nothing to do with felt heat or cold. Measurement, which is independent of our feelings, tells us how things are with respect to the water. It enables us to distinguish between what seems to be the case and what is the case. What is the case belongs to the external world, while what seems to be the case is in the mind. Secondary qualities do not allow a distinction between 'what is' and 'what seems to be'. We may contrast how the water feels on one occasion with how it feels on another occasion, but to call one of these 'the state of the water' seems arbitrary. Unlike the case of measurement, we do not seem able to break out from the realm of subjective opinion. Secondary qualities tell us nothing about the world.

These conclusions should remind us of our discussions in chapter 1, when we considered the view that only the measurable yields knowledge, while the senses yield only opinion. That view has influenced us when we want to distinguish between primary and secondary qualities. Historically, the view has been influenced by the achievements of physics, for which the primary qualities are of first importance. Secondary qualities are of no concern in

Galileo's experiments. When a ball rolls down an inclined plane, the colour of the ball, or the sound that it makes, are irrelevant. The properties which count are those which can be used in physical measurement. You may then go on to say that the shape, size and weight of the ball are its essential properties – the only real properties that it has – whereas its smell, colour and sound are not among its real qualities. This need not cause any difficulties as long as we realize that 'real' here means 'relevant to our present purposes'.

But some philosophers want to say more than this. They forget the contextual qualification and want to say, in absolute terms, that primary qualities tell us something about the external world whereas secondary qualities do not. No doubt the colour of the ball is of no interest in certain experiments, but does it follow from that fact that the ball does not have a real colour? Of course, in other contexts, the colour of the ball may be extremely important. The game of snooker comes readily to mind. And should someone ask us what is the colour of a ball in a box and we reply, 'Red', why should it be thought that we are not referring to the real colour of the ball? So there seems to be no reason for saying, in absolute terms, that primary qualities refer to the external properties of objects while secondary qualities do not.

More general considerations may lead us to distinguish between primary and secondary qualities.[2] It has been said that primary qualities, unlike secondary qualities, constitute what we mean by a physical object. This can be brought out by saying that if we cannot recognize primary qualities, it is hard to see how we could cope with our physical surroundings. A person's colour-blindness could go undetected. It need not impinge drastically on the rest of that person's life. Contrast this with what is implied by a person's failure to master the notion of size.

Consider a comparison between a jug and a glass. What could we do to establish the difference in size apart from measuring it? We could fill the jug with water, pour the water into the glass, and get the person to see that when the glass overflows, there is still water left in the jug. Again, if the jug and glass are put alongside each other, we can get a person to pass a hand over the top of the glass and find that it hits the side of the jug. Inability to recognize size, unlike colour-blindness, has these widespread ramifications. All of this may be true. It may explain, in part, the use of the terms 'primary' and 'secondary'. But it would in no way justify the absolute claims that primary qualities refer to the external world while secondary qualities do not, and that while primary qualities are in external objects, secondary qualities are in the mind.

Let us go back to the example of the water which feels hot to one hand and cold to another. That effect can be achieved by putting one hand in tepid water after it has been in cold water, and the other hand in the same water after it has been in hot water. The example is supposed to show that 'hot', 'cold' or 'tepid' cannot be said to be descriptions of the water. But have we not described water in precisely that way in setting up the example? We speak of a bowl of tepid water, and of hands which have been in hot and cold water. How are we able to do this? It is because we agree on what we mean by 'tepid', 'hot' and 'cold'. Our agreement is shown in our common reactions. If I put my hand under running water that we call 'hot', I will withdraw it quickly. Such reactions fix the meaning of 'hot' for us. The same is true in other cases. I may hold my hand under tepid water until I say 'It's cold now'. In both cases I expect the same reaction from anyone else whose hand is held under running water in the same circumstances. It is because of such agreements that plumbers are not thrown into hopeless confusion when asked to install hot and cold water. The fact that some person may be able to hold his hand under hot water without flinching simply serves to underline the norm. The person is the exception which proves the rule; the rule by which we can describe water as hot, cold or tepid.

It is important to recognize that within the ways in which we speak of secondary qualities, we have ways of distinguishing between what seems to be the case and what is the case, and between what is true of an object as opposed to being in the mind. But if philosophers say that secondary qualities do not belong to an object, or that they are in the mind, this obscures the possibility of these distinctions.

This can be illustrated in terms of the example of the water. The example explains why water which *was* tepid *seemed* hot to one hand and cold to another hand. What is the case and what seems to be the case is distinguished by reference to our normal reactions in these contexts. Think of a different example. While daydreaming, I place my hand under cold running water. For an instant, I think that the water is hot and jerk my hand away instinctively as if I had been scalded. It may be said that the experience of feeling hot water was not a real one, but something which was simply in my mind.

Within the ways in which we talk about colours, too, we have distinctions between what is the case and what seems to be the case.[3] It will not do, then, to say that colours belong to the realm of opinion, to what seems to be the case, but never to external objects. The pillar box may look orange under sodium lighting, but we do not say that it has changed its colour. We say that although the pillar-box *looks* orange, it *is* red. If the light in a tailor's shop is bad, we may take the material outside to appreciate its *real* colour. For a wide range of examples, what we mean by the 'real' colour of an object is how an object looks in daylight to people with normal eyesight. But this is not always so. By the 'real' colour of a woman's hair we mean its natural colour before she dyed it. So although the hair may *look* blonde in daylight to people with normal eyesight, we say that its *real* colour is brown. A fish which looks multi-coloured in its natural habitat may seem to be a dirty grey when out of the water. I suspect, in this case, that most people would say that the *real* colour of the fish is how it looks in its natural surroundings. But we are not always forced to say what is *the* colour of something. Think of a chameleon, the mountainside or the sky. In the case of taste, too, we have distinctions between what is the case and what seems to be the case. We say the water only *seems* to taste rough because we have been eating ice-cream before drinking it. Standard reactions are implied by the advice to clear the palate before tasting a wine which is a contrast to the one we have just tasted.

It would be hard to deny the centrality or variety of the distinctions we make within our talk of secondary qualities between what is in the object and what is in the mind, or between what is the case and what seems to be the case. As we have said, the way in which some philosophers distinguish between primary and secondary qualities obscures these distinctions from us. There are no good reasons for saying that secondary qualities are in the mind, or that they only inform us of appearances. But if we are to reject the philosophical distinction, it is important to see why it is made in the first place. A philosopher may be happy to accept our examples and argue, nevertheless, that there are features of them which show that his talk of secondary qualities is not pointless. It has been argued that if we look to these features of secondary qualities, which show that they are dispositional, relational and mental, we can see why it has been said that, strictly speaking, secondary qualities are not *in* objects. A stricter analysis of secondary qualities would show that what they are is *a power that objects possess* to create certain experiences in *us*. This is why secondary qualities can be said not to belong to external objects themselves. To assess this argument, we need to examine what is meant by the dispositional, relational and mental features of secondary qualities. In all three contexts, what is being said is that the analysis of secondary qualities cannot be done by reference simply to the objects to which they are attributed.

Consider the example of colour. What is meant by saying that this secondary quality is dispositional? This refers to the fact that to say that gold is yellow is to say that if I place myself in certain conditions in relation to gold, I am disposed to have certain sense-experiences, a visual field that we call 'yellow'. But my disposition to react in a certain way to the gold is not enough to account for our saying that the gold is yellow. That is why the second characteristic of secondary qualities, their relational character, is important.

Colour is a relational quality because my reaction to gold is related to factors other than the gold itself. There are not only the light conditions, but also the reactions of other people with normal eyesight in the same conditions to the gold. My reactions agree with the reactions of others.

The third characteristic of colour as a secondary quality is its being a mental experience. This refers to the visual field which each individual experiences in the conditions described. This experience is said to be a mental experience.

If we combine the three characteristics of secondary qualities, we can see why some philosophers have said that what we mean by 'yellow' is a certain power in objects to produce certain mental experiences in us. When I look at gold in certain conditions, I and others are disposed to have the mental experience that we call 'yellow'. Philosophers have concluded that, strictly speaking, we should not say that yellow is in the gold. Rather, we should say, metaphorically, that the yellow is *between* the gold and the class of normally sighted people. But is not this an odd conclusion? After all, the point of the analysis was to unpack the meaning of saying that 'gold is yellow'. Why should we be deterred from saying this by the fact that we see gold as yellow only in certain conditions, and if we have normal eyesight? To talk of the yellow being *between* the gold and the class of normally sighted people seems to have no clear meaning. It is at best a misleading way of saying that many factors are involved when we see gold as yellow.

Furthermore, what we have been told of the dispositional, relational and mental character of secondary qualities does not free us from the sceptical challenge that we met in previous chapters. Neither does the analysis free us from the temptation to say that secondary qualities are in the mind, rather than in external objects. Why should this be so?

Let us say that when I look at gold in certain light conditions, I am disposed to have a mental experience that I call 'yellow', if my eyesight is normal. It is said that I am having the *same* mental experience as other normally sighted people will have in the same conditions. Perhaps this is part of what is meant by saying that 'yellow' is between the gold and the class of normally sighted people. But the vital question concerns the sense in which we can speak of a *shared* experience in this context. The sceptic will ask how I know that the mental experience I am having is the *same* experience as other people are having. For all that has been said so far, I may be giving the description 'yellow' to a mental experience which is quite different from the experiences to which others give the same description.

The sceptical challenge of the last chapter returns. If each individual is the recipient of a mental experience, how is the identity of that experience established? How could it ever be known that this experience is the same as the experience others have? If 'yellow' is said to be *between* the gold and the class of normally sighted people, what kind of agreement exists between them?

There is one way of understanding the agreement which would lead us back to all the sceptical difficulties that we have met in the previous chapters. It may be thought that in saying that gold is yellow, we are referring to the way in which the majority of people react to the gold. On this view, individuals would know what mental experiences they are having prior to reaching majority agreement. Some individuals will have the mental experience 'orange' when they look at gold. Other individuals will have the mental experience 'green' when they look at gold. But the vast majority, when they look at gold, have the experience 'yellow'. They all agree to abide by the reactions of the majority. When we say 'Gold is yellow' we are referring to this majority view.

Such a view runs into difficulties that we have already encountered. It assumes that I could know what colour I am experiencing from my own case alone.[4] If I say that an object is yellow, I want my description to be correct. But the same is true of my description of my mental experience. After all, there is a difference between *thinking* that I am seeing or describing 'yellow', and actually seeing or describing 'yellow'. But, in order to make this distinction, there must be something *independent* of *my* experience against which it can be checked. But in the account we are offered, there is nothing independent of my mental experience against which any claims concerning it can be checked. The mental experience is supposed to inform me that it is 'seeing yellow'. But I can only know that I am seeing yellow if I also know what does not count as seeing yellow. To know that, there must be something other than my mental experience to appeal to. Since the account that we are offered allows for no such appeal, the distinction between sameness and difference does not even get off the ground.

The sceptical challenge remains. How can we ever know that we see the *same* colours? Perhaps our mental experiences are like coloured spectacles through which each of us sees colours differently. That analogy is a weak one. Talk of coloured spectacles trades on an agreement in the meaning of colours. When people take off their coloured spectacles, they will see the same colours as everyone else. No general scepticism can be arrived at from examples such as these. The same would be the case for such an attempt made on the basis of colour-blindness. Some cases of colour-blindness may be difficult to detect, but this difficulty cannot become inconceivability. Colour-blindness, so far from undermining our agreement about colours, underlines it.

But what is this agreement that we are appealing to? It is not the agreement of majority opinion which led us back to scepticism. The agreement in our colour reactions is not an agreement that was made at any time. Individuals react. They do not agree to react in the way that they do. They react and find, as a matter of brute fact, that they *agree in their reactions*. They do not agree to agree. So there is no agreement made on the basis of the private mental experiences in different individuals. Common concepts are not built up from these several private starting-points, the minds and their ideas, that we discussed in the last chapter. The reaction we call 'seeing yellow' is a common reaction, a shared reaction, from the outset. When this is appreciated, the necessary presupposition of the sceptical challenge is not granted. We do not begin as passive recipients of private intelligible mental experiences, faced with the problem of wondering how we can ever be justified, from this starting-point, in saying that there are common experiences that we share with others. The conclusion that we are trying to draw concerning agreement in reactions is a fundamental one. Let us consider it further in terms of some simple examples. Think of our reactions to what we call a bright light. We do not agree to react in the ways in which we do. We agree *in* our reactions. We are dazzled. We shade our eyes, avert our gaze, turn away, and so on. Think of our reactions to what we call 'bitter' and 'sweet'. We eat something very bitter by mistake: we may spit it out, make noises which express dislike, thrust it from us, and so on. Think of our reactions to pleasant and unpleasant smells. Once again, the agreement shows itself *in* our reactions.

But it is easy to miss how deeply significant it is to say this. It is easy to miss its importance. This has often been shown to be the case when someone is asked what would happen if this agreement in reactions did not occur. What if people's reactions were random? It is very tempting to reply by saying that, in that case, one person would see orange while another sees yellow; that while someone may see a bright light, someone else may see it as a dull light; that while a fruit will be bitter to one person it will be sweet to another; and so on. But that is precisely what *cannot* be said. To think otherwise would be to fall back into saying that the meaning of colours, tastes and smells are given in a person's private mental experience. If people's reactions were random, we could not describe them as random experiences of 'yellow', 'bright' and 'bitter', since the very possibility of these notions depends on the reactions *not being random*. Without the agreement in reactions, talk of colours, tastes and smells has no meaning. We have to remember what we would be asked to imagine. We would have to imagine some people being dazzled by what we now call a bright light, while others would stare unflinchingly into it. We have to imagine some reacting with revulsion to what we call a bitter taste, while others smile and exhibit the kind of reactions we now show in relation to sweet things. Extending the examples, we have to think of people putting their hands on what we call red-hot oven plates and showing no more concern than we show in resting our hands on a desk. The random reactions involve nothing less than the break-up of our familiar surroundings in which talk of our experiences has its sense. We cannot describe the random experiences as randomly 'seeing yellow', 'seeing a bright light', 'having a bitter taste' or 'experiencing an unpleasant smell', since these descriptions depend on the possibility of common reactions which the random reactions rule out. Since our ordinary circumstances are constituted by these common reactions, the absence of such reactions means the absence of such circumstances. If there are no common reactions, we have no life in common. We would have the meaningless concatenation of sensory data we talked of in the last chapter.

The agreement in reactions that we are talking about is not only essential for agreement in judgements. It is also essential in understanding negation, disagreement in judgement and a radical inability to judge. Unless there were a distinction between the meaning that a certain experience has and what I am experiencing at a given moment, I could not know that the experience is of a certain colour, taste or smell. What is independent of my experience at a given time is the meaning fixed by the common reactions which determine our use of 'yellow', 'bitter', 'pungent', and so on. This independence enables me to say, at any given time, that I am *not* seeing yellow, tasting anything bitter or smelling anything unpleasant.

Agreement in reactions is essential in making our disagreements possible. We could not disagree over whether a certain object is yellow unless we agreed about the meaning of 'yellow'. That meaning is presupposed in the disagreement. Otherwise, what is the disagreement about?

Agreement in reactions also explains the fate of individuals cut off from it. They are cut off from the possibility of judgement. Blindness is an obvious example in the case of colours. But think also of cases in which the reactions of an individual are random with respect to crying out, smiling, looking, and so on. The individual is at the mercy of these reactions. If such reactions pervade much of the person's life, it becomes a vegetative state. In the case of more restricted examples of lack of agreement, such as when a person gives out agonized cries in the *absence* of any pain or discomfort, our agreed reactions mark such a person off as the strange one; cut off, in certain respects, from a common life. We shall say more about this in chapter 5.

We can now see how essential it is to understand *the kind* of agreement involved when we speak of our agreement in reactions where secondary qualities are concerned. It is not an agreement that we make with the majority. On such a view, the individual is set in radical opposition to the world. When placed in certain conditions in relation to gold, the individual is said to have a certain mental experience called 'seeing yellow'. We then inherit all the difficulties we have discussed about how it can ever be determined that two individuals ever have *the same* experience. Further, how does the individual know, on such a view, what experience is being received? We are told that once the mind receives its sensory data, these are named. As we have seen, however, on such a view, how can we ever know that the sense-datum is given the right name? Among the data the mind is said to receive are said to be different qualities, some primary and others secondary. The latter are said to be, not in objects, but in the mind. Alternatively, they are said to be powers in objects to cause mental experiences in us. We have seen that there is no good reason to speak in this way. On the view presented, we are still faced with the sceptical challenge of showing how, from the starting-point of the passive mind and its ideas, we can ever be justified in speaking of an external world.

In emphasizing the importance of our common *reactions*, we have presented not a passive, but an *active* self; a self which is not a passive recipient of data, but active *in the world*. In one of the most primitive of our reactions, namely, reaching out, we have the beginnings of a direction between ourselves and what surrounds us. This is a distinction realized in the world, not in a passive subject set over against it.

In a striking metaphor, perception has been called the dance of the body.[5] Think of our discussion of secondary qualities in the light of this metaphor: the common reactions in which the distinction between bright and dull has its sense – the dance of the eyes; the common reactions in which the distinction between bitter and sweet has its sense – the dance of the tongue; the common reactions in which rough and smooth has it sense – the dance of the hands. All of these reactions, set in the context of other characteristic reactions of the human body, can be seen as a kind of dance. And the dance is a common dance.

In this common dance, we cannot be seen as solitary individuals locked in the private, experiential data of our own minds. We are not faced, therefore, with the sceptical issues which depend on this confused conception of ourselves. We may have good reason, in certain contexts, for distinguishing between primary and secondary qualities, but no good reason for making an absolute distinction between them, by saying that whereas primary qualities are in external objects, secondary qualities are in the mind. As we have seen, in relation to primary and secondary qualities, we can make a distinction between what is the case and what seems to be the case.

In resisting the attempt to drive a sceptical wedge between sense-data and external objects, between qualities and things, we have spoken about the agreement in reactions between human beings. I and others share these reactions. But not a great deal has been said yet concerning this 'I' or the other human beings with whom it is said to share a common life. These will be the topics of the next two chapters.

4

Mind, Brain and Self

The sceptical challenge that we have encountered in the previous chapters invoked a picture of two realms: on the one hand, the mind and its ideas; and on the other hand, the external world. The challenge was to show how, from the starting-point of the former, we can ever be justified in claiming to know the latter. The mind, on this account, is regarded as the passive recipient of its ideas. In this reference to 'the mind', we are talking impersonally. But if we referred to our own experience we should have to say that *I* am the passive recipient of ideas, since, on this account, I am identified with my mind.

But what is this 'I' which is being referred to? For the view presented, this question becomes a difficult one. By the 'I' is meant my 'self', but what does *that* mean? It certainly does not mean 'my body'. I say 'My body is tall' or 'My body is injured', but not 'My body thinks' or 'My body wills'. I think and I will, but the 'I' seems to be a vague something that I cannot locate. I can locate features of my body by perception: by looking at the colour of my hair, the complexion of my skin, the wounds on my hands, and so on. But we cannot locate the 'I' by perception. Instead, it has been suggested that we locate it by introspection, by looking inside ourselves. This will reveal the 'I' which some have described as pure consciousness. But this is where the embarrassment becomes acute. No such mental identity can be found. I reflect on my ideas, but I do not find in addition to them, or underlying them, some extra something called the self or consciousness. And yet I want to say that all these ideas are *mine*, that *I* am experiencing them, and so on. These results are often reported as if they were the results of an empirical search. Introspection discovers no pure consciousness. Among the ideas of my mind it discovers no idea of the self. And yet all these ideas are mine. The mind is myself. Clearly, what is presented as though it were the result of an empirical search is really a conceptual investigation into the meaning of 'the self'. In an attempt to solve this puzzle, some philosophers turned in a direction which we have already met in this essay. If consciousness is not an entity underlying my ideas, or something in which all the ideas are contained, then it must be a function of the ideas themselves. There must be a something about the ideas themselves which tells me that they are mine. Consciousness of the self is somehow contained in the ideas. I am related to my ideas and experiences in a way in which no one else can be. I have privileged access to my ideas. Consciousness is this enjoyment of my ideas and experiences.

But this view runs into familiar difficulties. What answer does it give to the question: How do I know who I am? There is no difficulty in seeing how I am identified by others. I am picked out as this person from among others. The distinction between myself and others is essential for the notion of identity. But that is exactly what the appeal to consciousness cannot give me. How am I to be picked out as this consciousness from among others? I cannot be picked out because, on the view we are considering, I am not acquainted with other consciousnesses. I am said to be acquainted with a consciousness that contains a knowledge of myself and others. The problem is in seeing how this claim can mean anything. If I am pure consciousness, there is no question of selecting my consciousness out as one among many. Consciousness is supposed to inform me who I am. But, as we have seen, I can only have an identity by contrast with others. It follows, then, that if I am pure consciousness, I cannot know who I am.[1]

How do we get into these difficulties? We have said that there is no difficulty in seeing how others identify me. They pick me out from among others. But that is something others need to do. I do not need to pick out myself to tell myself who I am. Of course, I often pick myself out for the sake of others. The chairman may ask, 'Is anyone angry about this proposal?' and I reply, 'I am'. Again, the dentist may ask, 'Who is in acute pain here?' and I reply, 'I am'. But I do not need to pick myself out in order to inform myself that I am angry or in pain. This fact feeds the view that consciousness informs me, infallibly, that I am in pain and angry. At the same time, I am informed infallibly about who I am.

We can see that this notion of pure consciousness is the notion of the mind and its ideas that we met in previous chapters. The individual cannot be sure of anything outside the immediate ideas and experiences which constitute consciousness. As we shall see in the next chapter, on this view, there can be no certainty concerning the existence of other human beings. But in the present chapter, we see that this view cannot provide us with an intelligible notion of the self or of self-identity. On the other hand, what are we to make of the fact that I do not have to pick myself out to tell myself who I am? Does this mean that awareness of the self is something independent of a human neighbourhood?

Some philosophers have argued that when I say 'I am in pain', I am picking out the same person as you pick out when you say, 'He is in pain'.[2] This is certainly true when I am giving information to others about my pain. After I have told the doctor, 'I am in pain', the doctor informs the nurse that I am in pain by saying, 'He is in pain'. The same person is being referred to. But think of occasions when I am alone and mutter, 'I am in pain'. Do I pick myself out for my own benefit on such occasions? Am I informing myself that I am in pain? Obviously not. What, then, does the expression 'I am in pain' amount to? It is not a report on my pain, but replaces a natural expression of it, such as a cry. But it is essential to realize that I do not learn the concept of pain from my natural expression of it alone. I am born into a human neighbourhood in which people exhibit natural expressions of pain to which others react sympathetically or unsympathetically. In the neighbourhood, we are constantly interchanging as people who express pain and who observe the pain of others. In this interchange, I do not observe my own pain. Nevertheless, my sense of pain, and my identity as a person, depend on these interrelations in the human neighbourhood. We shall have more to say of this in the next chapter. The point, at the moment, is to see that the fact that I do not observe my pain, or report on it when I say, 'I am in pain', does not lead to the conclusion that I come to know what pain or my identity is from my state alone. A pure consciousness does not inform me of these notions. I am not a mind locked in its ideas, problematically related to any world wider than itself. I have my identity as a person among others in a human neighbourhood. Within this neighbourhood, where pain, anger, joy, and intentions of various kinds are concerned, I am constantly interchanging between third person uses of language where I refer to persons, their states and actions, and first person uses which, in various ways, are modes of self-expression.

At this point, however, a new direction is taken by some philosophers. They applaud the philosophical dissolution of the idea of the mind and its ideas. They regard this as a piece of mystification well lost. They also applaud the emphasis on the human neighbourhood, and the interrelationships, not between bodiless minds, but between human beings. But they do not think that our intellectual curiosity should be content to rest there. Do we not want to know how this life in the human neighbourhood is possible? Although our starting-point may be the psychological terms that we employ from day to day, these cannot be the terminus of our investigations. We must ask, aided by science, what are the conditions and ultimate explanations of the life that we share with each other. The direction in which we have to look is actually provided by the colloquial answer we receive if we ask people what thinking is. They would reply: something that goes on in the brain. When we praise people for their activities, no matter how diverse, we say that they have a good brain. Common-sense tells us that the brain is the home of thinking. Of course, it is up to science to provide the more technical details, to tell us how the thinking which goes on in the brain makes possible the rich and varied activities in which we share.

At first, it may seem that there is a major difference between the philosophical proposal that we are considering now, and the dualism between the mind and the external world that we have discussed already. In the one case, the starting-point is the mind and its ideas, whereas, in the other case, the starting-point is our ordinary human neighbourhood and our relations with each other. But the difference is more apparent than real. In the dualistic picture of the mind and the external world, we are asked to justify how we can know of the existence of the latter, given that the former is our necessary starting-point. In the present proposal, the journey is from our familiar surroundings to an explanation of them in terms of the internal workings of the brain. In both cases, the ordinary world that we share is said to be a function of something more fundamental than itself: in the one case, the mind and its ideas; in the other case, the brain and its operations. We shall find that the problems which beset the dualism of the mind and the external world now beset the dualism of the brain and the external world. We were faced with the task of showing how perception, memory and imagination could be accounted for in terms of the qualities of the mind's ideas. We are now faced with the task of showing how perception, memory and imagination can be accounted for in terms of the physical states and operations of the brain. The challenge has a familiar ring: How can we speak of the familiar surroundings we know in terms of inner mental events or physical events, found in minds or brains, their respective homes? The answer to the second challenge may turn out to be the answer to the first: to reject the assumptions on which the challenge is based.

Those who regard the familiar world in which we move as awaiting a scientific explanation, tend to regard that world as a very complex system. Simple examples are offered to help us understand this. Think of a washing machine. It has the sub-functions of soaking, soaping, agitating, rinsing and spinning. Sub-functions can be broken down into sub-sub-functions until we hit on structural bits which are actually responsible for some specific function. No structural item alone can account for the overall effect we want to explain, but all the structural items, working together, can do so. In the case of the washing machine, the soap dispenser, the pump, the thermostat, the drum, and so on, all have specific functions which collectively – but not singly – wash the clothes. Could we not look on the brain in the same way? Through a breakdown of functions into sub-functions and sub-sub-functions, could we not also arrive at some structural items which would account for some low-level function of the brain? Collectively, but not singly, the hope is that these low-level functions will account for the ordinary activities that we share with each other. The hope is for a science of human behaviour, a cognitive science.

We can appreciate the fascination that such a hope has for us. Our ordinary psychological terms, such as 'thinking', 'believing', 'seeing', 'remembering' and 'imagining', while said to be perfectly adequate for our everyday purposes, are vague and difficult to make systematic. What if it were possible to decode these activities into a more basic structural language which would explain their nature and possibility to us? In such explanations, all anthropomorphism would have to be avoided. This has not always been avoided in psychological explanations. The brain has been described as 'receiving messages, 'decoding', 'translating', and so on. These are the very activities that the physical states and operations of the brain were meant to explain. By attributing them to the brain, it is as if we were postulating 'a little man' at work there.

If we could arrive at structural–functional explanations, it is said, we could arrive at a physicalism which would avoid such anthropomorphisms. Just as we do not have to say that water-heating is washing, although it is part of it, so we do not have to say that neuron-firing in the brain is seeing, although it is part of it. In the case of the washing machine, we say that structural items, collectively, but not singly, account for the washing of clothes. Neurons firing – along with other brain processes – collectively, but not singly, account for all our thinking.[3]

But at this point, a philosophical worry surfaces. No matter how many brain processes we appeal to, how, on the basis of non-conscious events, such as neurons firing, do we ever arrive at conscious acts such as seeing, remembering, imagining, and so on? Does not the difficulty have a familiar ring? Are we not back at the sceptical challenges that we have already met? How, from the mind and its ideas, can we ever give an account of perception, memory and imagination? How, on the basis of physical events in the brain, can we give an account of the same activities? In both cases, the starting-points offered are fatally cut off from the ordinary surroundings in which these activities have their sense. This is because, in both philosophical perspectives, the assumption is made that these ordinary surroundings are irrelevant to the essence of cognitive activity and, therefore, to the essence of who we really are. In the one case, the essence of the self and its cognitive activity is said to be the mind. In the other case, this essence is said to be the brain. The familiar appearances of the human beings among whom we live our lives thus become inessential accompaniments of these essences.

We saw in the case of the dualism between the mind and the external world that the reverse is the case. The same is true in the case of the brain. When I perceive colours, tell others about them or imagine them in their absence, I do so without the slightest knowledge of any processes going on in my brain, or the brains of other people. Our ordinary understandings of each other are quite independent of such knowledge. Yet, if the essence of these understandings and activities is said to reside in the brain, then they should not be lost to us even if our ordinary surroundings were absent. Since these surroundings are inessential, we would preserve the essence of who we are in their absence.

To illustrate this claim, the following example has been advanced. It is assumed that when physiological technology is sufficiently refined, it will be possible to keep a human brain alive *in vitro*. It is said that since the brain will have already learned a language before it was put *in vitro*, it will be able to think verbally in its disembodied state. It will be able to participate in any cognitive activity.

If this suggestion is taken seriously, it becomes the basis of a bizarre sceptical challenge. If all the familiar experiences of my life are, in essence, brain states and activities, how do I know that that is not what I am – a brain preserved in a vat? Again, the sceptical challenge should sound familiar. How do I know that I am more than a mind and its ideas, and that there is an external world independent of me? How do I know that I am more than a brain and its processes, and that there is an external world independent of me?[4]

The brain-in-a-vat hypothesis is presented as though it were a serious hypothesis. What if attempts are made to answer it in experimental terms? Here are two experiments which have been offered in the discussion.[5] First, imagine a brain alive *in vitro* placed next to the body from which it has been removed. Let us suppose that we can locate a process in the brain which has been correlated with 'hearing a buzzing sound' in living persons. Does it follow that when we do so the body from whom the brain has been removed hears a buzzing sound? Not at all, since the person is dead. Does the brain hear the buzzing sound? Not at all, since the buzzing sound that we are talking about is a sound heard by living people. We do not know what it means to speak of a brain hearing a buzzing sound.

In the second experiment, the body, as well as the brain which has been removed from it, is kept alive. The brain is stimulated so that it is in the state which corresponds to the experience of 'remembering a walk one has returned from five minutes ago' in living persons. When the brain is restored to the body, the person claims to have had the experience of remembering going for a walk. Does it now follow that either the person or the brain has remembered something? All that follows in the case of the person is that a brain which has been stimulated in a certain way, when replaced, creates a delusion that the person has had an experience that the person has never had. As we saw in chapter 2, whether we are remembering something cannot be determined by the quality of a mental experience. Nor can it be determined by a physical state or operation of the brain. We can only speak of the person having a 'memory' of going for a walk, by placing the word in inverted commas to indicate that it is not a real memory. A person cannot remember going for a walk if that person has not been for a walk. As for the brain having such a memory, we do not know what that would mean. Brains do not go on walks and therefore cannot remember going on walks.

The point of these two examples, deliberately cast in experimental form, is to indicate that what is really happening in them is a conceptual rejection of the brain-in-a-vat hypothesis. In both cases, we see that the vital consideration is that the brain-in-a-vat does not resemble a human being and does not lead a human life. The brain does not hear anything. It does not hear the distant sound of a bus; it does not peer at a distant corner in anticipation of the bus' appearance, nor remember that it was late yesterday or wonder whether it will be late again today. The brain does not grieve at the loss of a loved one, or share in the joy of good news. The brain does not have a body which doubles up in pain, or a face which can look happy, sad, radiant, bored, annoyed, and so on. These are examples of the ordinary circumstances of our lives which reference to the physical states and operations of the brain was meant to explain. But when we sever the notions of 'hearing', 'remembering', 'thinking', 'seeing' and 'imagining', from these circumstances, we sever them from their meaning in our lives at the same time.

It is comic when these conceptual reminders are treated as though they were experimental confirmations of the lives that we lead. For example, it has been said that there is overwhelming evidence against the brain-in-a-vat hypothesis. If I am sitting in a chair writing on sheets of paper, I do not feel like a brain-in-a-vat. I do not think of myself as a brain-in-a-vat. I know that whatever I say will be re-described as an experience being had by a brain-in-a-vat. But this supposition is itself irrational, since the consensus in my experiences, the pattern that they have, shows me that I am not a brain-in-a-vat.

Is there not something crazy in this picture of us checking that we are not brains-in-vats? In the appeal to the pattern of our experiences, we see the re-emergence of the view that the consensus in our experiences tells us when we are in contact with reality; when we are seeing an apple and not imagining one, for example. But, as we have already said, no matter what pattern in my experiences I invoke, this is consistent with the apple not existing. The appeal to such an experimental pattern does not show that I am not a brain-in-a-vat. But this time we have to add that nothing either shows or does not show *that*. This does not leave it an open question. It shows it to be an unintelligible one. We are not offering counter-evidence against a genuine hypothesis. Rather, we are showing why the lives that we share with each other, do not allow us to give sense to the suggestion. We cannot give it any purchase.

The attempts to locate the essence of the self and its experiences either in a mind and its ideas, or in a brain and its states and operations, suffer from the same defect. They cut off the self and its experiences from the human neighbourhood in which they have their life and meaning. That neighbourhood is one I share with other human beings. In the next chapter, we examine the consequences of attempts to cut off not the self, but other human beings, from such a neighbourhood.

5

The Self and Others

The sceptic asks us to think of the individual as a solitary mind, the passive recipient of experiential data. As we have seen, the sceptic asks how, on the basis of such data, the individual can ever be sure of the existence of an external world. That external world is said to include the existence of other human beings. But the mind is only acquainted with its *own* data. No other mind can appear among such data. The sceptical challenge is obvious: If I am locked in the experiential data of my own mind, how can I ever be sure of the existence of other minds?

Since my acquaintance with other human beings cannot be immediate, I simply *believe* that they exist. I cannot *know* that they exist. But what reasons can I give for my belief? It seems that I must infer the existence of other human beings from the data of my own experience. How do I do this? Consider the example of pain. I am acquainted immediately with my own pain, but I am not acquainted in the same way with anyone else's pain. I do not find out that I am in pain. I simply have pain. But I do find out that others are in pain. I observe that they are in pain from features of their behaviour. But how do I know which features to look for? I choose those features which accompany my own pain. When I am in pain, I may make certain gestures, such as doubling-up, grimacing or holding my stomach. So when I see someone else making these same gestures, I conclude, by analogy, that that person must be in pain too. My belief must take this form, since whereas I am in a privileged position with respect to my own pain, I cannot enjoy that position with respect to anyone else's pain. All I see is the outward manifestations of the pain.

This analogical argument is a very weak one. It is important to note that in my own case I do not know I am in pain from observing my own facial or bodily movements. According to the view that we are considering, the self is identified with the mind. The mind has full knowledge of pain and, indeed, of joy, anger, and so on, quite independently of any bodily actions which may encounter these experiences. The body does not belong to the essence of the self. But if my own bodily behaviour is not essentially linked to my experience of pain, it follows that what I observe in others is also inessential to the experience. The regularity of the connection between my pain and features of my bodily behaviour may impress me, but from this one case alone how can I be confident that the same connection exists in others? For all I know, the outward behaviour of others may accompany experiences of quite a different kind, or may not accompany any experience at all. How can I ever know?

We have presented the sceptical challenge in terms of pain, but the challenge is far more fundamental than this one example would suggest. In my own case, my privileged position from which I enjoy my experiences is identified as being my mind. My body is the outer shell within which my mind resides. I can observe the behaviour of my own body, as I observe the behaviour of other bodies. But in the case of others, this is all I observe. I have no direct acquaintance with other minds. Of course, as in the case of pain, I can attempt to argue by analogy. Since there is a mind behind my outward behaviour, I assume that there are minds behind the same behaviour by other bodies. But this analogical argument inherits all the weaknesses that it had in the case of pain. At best, all that can be said is that the existence of other minds is probable. It certainly makes sense to wonder and even to doubt whether inner selves do reside within the external bodies that I observe. The sceptical challenge can certainly take an extreme form: How can I ever know that I am not the only human being, and that the others who surround me are not mere automatons?[1]

How are we to come to grips with these sceptical arguments? The suggestion that everyone except myself may be an automaton may have an eerie fascination, but what does this possibility imply? It involves the assumption that there are no inner selves within the bodies that I perceive. It also involves the assumption that there is no essential relation between the behaviour that I observe and the experiences enjoyed by human minds. The experiences of pain, joy, anger, and so on, are complete and lose nothing in the absence of any outward behaviour. We have to try to imagine what kind of situation would be realized if these assumptions were taken seriously.

We may think, at first, that there is no difficulty whatever in making a distinction between the experiences of pain, anger, fear, joy, and so on, and their natural expression in outward behaviour. We are probably thinking of situations such as the following: 'Although the pain in his side was acute, he managed to conceal it from his mother who had popped in for a few moments to see how he was. The coming of such pain, he had been told, would be one of the first signs of his worsening condition and he did not want her to know before she had to'; 'He was happy when his son told him that his relationship with his girlfriend was over, but he managed to keep a smile from his face in case his son misunderstood the reason for his relief'; 'Inside he was boiling with rage, but outwardly he maintained a calm countenance, determined that they should not have the satisfaction of seeing what effect their actions had had on him.' In these examples, we have a contrast between normal expressions of pain, happiness and anger, and their suppression for one reason or another. But in them, the natural expressions are contingently absent. The effort taken to suppress them itself shows that the connection between them and the experiences of pain, happiness and anger is not a contingent one.

But we would have to imagine something far more extreme to imagine situations in which the suggestions of scepticism would be realized. In them, the separation between experiences and their natural expressions would have to be a radical one, not merely contingent. How are we to imagine this? Perhaps we could just about conjure up a scene in the seclusion of our study. We could picture human beings moving about stiffly like robots. Out of their mouths would come words like, 'I am happy to see you', 'I am in agony' or 'I am angry'. But these words would not be accompanied by any of the behavioural surroundings that we would normally expect in such circumstances. What would we make of these words?

Again, we may think that these situations are similar to other examples which may come to mind. I call unexpectedly on someone who greets me stonily, but says, 'So glad to see you'. If someone is asked, 'Do you want to come to the fair?' and replies in a flat monotone, 'Yes, I do', the retort may be, 'Look, do you want to come or not?' But why the retort if the answer 'Yes' has already been achieved? Was it not the absence of any natural expression accompanying the words which led to the doubt about how the words were to be taken? But this lack of expression may be due to lack of sincerity or lack of interest which, of course, have natural expressions of their own. It can be contrasted with genuine expressions of sincerity and interest.

Scepticism asks us to imagine far more radical examples than these. The meaning of experiences, it seems, is given in the activity of the minds which have them. The natural expressions add nothing to the experiences. There need be nothing conceptually odd, therefore, in a radical divorce between experiences and their natural expressions. But if there were such a divorce, we would not know how to take the words – we could make nothing of them. This suggests that the relation between words and their natural expressions is not a contingent one. It is in this context of these natural expressions that our talk of pain, anger, fear, happiness, and so on, have their sense. The sceptical challenge assumes that the connection between words and natural expressions can be broken. It suggests that although these natural expressions may be present, no self lies behind them. For all we know, the expressions might emerge from an automaton.

Once again, in the seclusion of a study, we can try to imagine a situation in which there is no connection between language and expressive behaviour. Imagine a person saying, 'I am extremely excited about winning the football pools', but showing no enthusiasm of any kind. Imagine someone saying, 'I am in sheer agony. I cannot stand the pain' without showing any sign of distress and while moving effortlessly among people, smiling, chatting, and so on. Imagine someone saying 'Fire' as a house becomes ablaze, but remaining completely passive, doing nothing. Now try to imagine some examples of such dislocations as a pervasive phenomenon in human life. People say that they are going, but do not move. People give reasons why an argument is thoroughly confused, but then conclude that it must be accepted as a result. People say that it is bitterly cold, and so decide to go out without any kind of coat. What could we make of these words? Nothing whatsoever. The words have no meaning because they have been cut off from expressive behaviour, actions, reactions, and so on, in which they have their sense. The words have no life because they have been cut off from life, the life in which they have their purchase and their sense. The important point is that this is the kind of madness we have to imagine if we want to give a credible picture of a dislocation between words and expressive behaviour.

But the sceptical suggestion is far more weird. When the sceptic argues that there is no internal connection between mental experiences of pain, anger, fear, and so on, and their behavioural expressions, we are *not* being asked to imagine the kind of scenes that we may conjure up in the seclusion of the study. On the contrary, we are asked to imagine that in the day-to-day circumstances of our lives, in all our dealings with others, they could turn out to be automatons. Unsurprisingly, we find that we simply cannot sustain this picture. We cannot sustain it when we are confronted by someone doubling-up as a result of a kick in a stomach. We cannot sustain it on witnessing a person's anger on discovering a burglar at home. We cannot sustain it when we see a person's terrified efforts to escape from a burning house. We cannot sustain it as we watch children at play.

The sceptic may not be impressed by these considerations. The inability to sustain the possibility that the people around are automatons may be said to be a *psychological* impossibility. But a psychological impossibility, it will be argued, is not a *logical* impossibility. We may not be able to sustain the possibility in practice, but it still makes sense to say that all the people around me – men, women and children – could be automatons. This response by the sceptic is misplaced. Our difficulty is not merely psychological. Our difficulty is in making any sense of what we are asked to imagine. This is because our sense of the human is rooted in the context of the actions and reactions that I have described. Consider the following bizarre example. Suppose that on a beach I notice a small key in a friend's back. Do I begin imagining, immediately, that my friend may be a robot? Perhaps I have been seeing too many films about humanoids. Perhaps the story that enfolds may lead to the conclusion that my friend is one of them. It would have to be quite a story. If the friend is of long standing, one I have been involved with in innumerable ways, what does the suggestion amount to? I can make nothing of it. But what about the key? Well, what about it? How it got there may remain a mystery. The important point is how the significance of the key is to be assessed. It is not the key which determines our practice, but our practice which determines the significance of the key. If the *only* difference in my relationship with my friend is the discovery of the key, then our practice, our human neighbourhood, would rob the suggestion that my friend is a robot of any sense.

The sceptical position relies, in fact, on a conception of the self that we have already rejected. Despite the presence of the human neighbourhood, we are to suppose that behind the behaviour we witness and share in, there are only robots. This is to entertain a conception of a private, isolated self cut off from the human neighbourhood. But it is that neighbourhood which gives us our sense of the human. We are born into that neighbourhood. In it, for example, there are characteristic reactions to pain and expressions of pain. We share a life with others in which we see and learn of the extremities of agonizing pain, alongside knowledge of the slightest twinges; we are acquainted with exaggerations concerning pain and with fortitude shown in suffering. The same point can be made for other cases. We are acquainted with people getting angry because they have been offended in many ways. We see people's gladness at receiving good news and their dismay at receiving bad news. We see them apprehensive in uncertainty. Without this shared life our talk of our human experiences makes no sense. In this shared life, the self is not the passive recipient of experiences into which scepticism turns it.

But neither is the self the reflector on abstract possibilities, the abstract possibility that the beings we see around us may be automatons. On such a view, we react to others as we do because we first believe that they are human beings. But such a belief is completely vacuous, since it is our characteristic actions and reactions which determine our sense of the human. An amusing example illustrates the grotesque results which intellectualism can lead to in this context. A philosopher argued that he came to the conclusion that he was living with another human being in the following way. On coming home from work he found a table laid for tea, his slippers warming at the fire, and so on. He argued that since these were the kind of preparations he would make were he to welcome someone home, he could justifiably infer that a human being must have made these preparations for him. What an odd argument this is, and it would become even odder if applied to the actual appearance of his wife, his conversation with her, his sexual relations with her, and so on. But even accepting it in the context in which it is presented gives us no reason for agreeing with it. He is able to recognize the welcome, not by any form of inferential argument, but because he was born into a family which is itself placed in a wider community. It is in such a context that we become acquainted with going to work, returning home, acts of welcome, and so on. An inferred wife expresses the craziness of intellectualism, a craziness appreciated by the way in which it distorts the interplay between human beings in the life we share with each other.

It may be argued that in emphasizing this common life that we share, our common actions and reactions, I have glossed over the greatest difference between oneself and others. I have my life to live and you have your life to live. One's life cannot be reduced to the lives of others. Surely, this is the essential difference which leads people to talk of one's privileged access in relation to one's own experiences. It is this essential difference which leads to the view that I cannot experience anyone else's pain, and that no one else can experience my pain. A picture is presented of each individual locked within his or her pain, with no possibility of shared experience. Are we not back with the scepticism that we have been arguing against?

We have already noted differences between what we can say of the pain of others, and what we can say of our own pains. I find out that others are in pain, but I do not find out that I am in pain. But although this distinction is perfectly sound, misleading conclusions may be drawn from it. It does not follow that I acquire the concept of pain from having a pain, any more than I acquire the concept 'red' simply by being confronted by a red patch.

I am born into a community in which certain actions and reactions already exist, actions and reactions in which I share. Some of these actions are unlearned. From my earliest years, if I am hurt I cry. Others show sympathy towards me. If I am about to fall, other reach out to prevent it. Should they fail, I am held, comforted with soothing words, and so on. It is in contexts such as these that we come to learn what pain is. I participate in a context in which these reactions are directed to me, and I react in similar ways to others. If these actions and reactions were modified in a radical way, it would be a modification of our concept of pain at the same time. For example, think of a tribe who share our pain reactions only when wounds are visible. In these circumstances, the wounded person exhibits all the signs of painful suffering that we do, while others react sympathetically in ways familiar to us. But where wounds are not visible, these actions and reactions are absent. A person may grimace and double-up in the way that we associate with pain behaviour, but does not regard this as being in pain. Neither does the person expect sympathetic reactions from others; nor are they given. It is tempting to say that, despite the absence of these actions and reactions, the person is undoubtedly in pain. If by this it is meant that *we* should say that the person is in pain, that is not in dispute. What else could we say? But the members of the tribe do not say this. If in saying that the person is in pain, we are claiming a judgement which is independent of our judgements and those of the tribe, this is confused. The assumption is that, independent of all reactions, the sensation will somehow announce its own identity as 'pain'. But, as we have seen elsewhere in this essay, our supposition is senseless. Until we have common actions and reactions there is no conception of pain. Its sense is rooted in the context of the expressive actions of the sufferer and the sympathetic responses of others, a context in which there are interchanges between being sufferer or sympathizer. We are receivers and givers of sympathy. This is the situation into which I am born, in which I learn the difference between 'I am in pain' and 'You are in pain'. Thus I do not recognize the sufferings of others by consulting my own case. If I witness a car crash, and see people lying around after it, moaning and groaning, I do not recognize what I see by analogical reasoning from my own case. I recognize it immediately as a scene in the common life that I share with others. I do not refer to my own case at all. It remains true, however, that I do not observe that I am in pain. 'I am in pain', it might be said, replaces a cry of pain. Pity, concern and compassion, it might be said, are forms which the conviction that someone is in pain may take.

Similar conclusions can be drawn in the case of anger, gladness, fear, and so on. I do not consult myself to see anger in another's face, in order to see the radiant gladness there, or in order to see the boredom, the apprehension or the terror. I do not see facial contortions from which I infer these states. No, I see the face immediately as angry, bored or sad. These observations, without inference, are possible in a common life that I share with others. Thus I may be as certain of your anger, your boredom and your fear as I am of my own.

These conclusions may seem disappointing. They seem to take all the mystery out of our relations with each other. Everyone seems to have been made an open book to everyone else, something that hardly accords with our experience. The emphasis on a common life seems to have made life all too commonplace. These misgivings have a point, and must be taken seriously.

Somehow or other, we must allow room for the notion of another person's life as something I can never know completely. Unless we do this, there will be an understandable disappointment with our conclusions. Let us see how this comes about.

It is easy to begin from the conviction that we are all strangers to each other for the most part. It is no accident that if asked how many close friends we have, it is extremely unlikely that we need more than the fingers of our hands to count them. What would we make of someone who claimed to have a hundred close friends? These familiar facts have led many to speak of the distance between human beings. People are often enigmas to each other. What if in an attempt to alleviate this conviction I appeal to the arguments of this chapter? Would they not be disappointing?

If the arguments are sound, they have shown what is wrong with the view that the necessary starting-point in our thinking about human beings is a private, solitary self, the passive receiver of sensory data. The arguments also show that we are not faced with the task of finding some analogical or inferential bridge from this starting-point to the conviction that other human beings exist. The supposition that I can never be sure that human beings could not turn out to be automatons was shown to be senseless.

Let us say that these conclusions are sound. What effect do they have on those concerned about the distances between human beings? Would they not amount to a highly comic response to the worry? Suppose that someone is depressed and despondent at the distances which separate people morally and emotionally. Would it be any form of reassurance if a philosopher were to retort, 'I can assure you that these others are human beings. They are certainly not automatons'?[2]

If it did make sense to say that certain 'human beings' turned out to be automatons, those concerned about distances between human beings would not have *their* worries answered by these cases. They have their worries *as members of a human community*. But it is a community which disappoints them. They hope that our sense of the human could be something more that it apparently is. Saying that human beings are not automatons is hardly a step in the direction of improving this sense. This sense of disappointment may be expressed in this way:

> What you have combatted in this chapter is a certain philosophical notion of privacy or a philosophical notion of loneliness. According to these notions I can never be sure of the existence of human beings other than myself. You have offered objections to this philosophical scepticism, and I am prepared to accept that they are successful. But these arguments against a philosophical conception of privacy and loneliness say nothing about real privacy and loneliness. Getting rid of the distances that philosophy has created between human beings, is not to get rid of real distances between human beings. The problem of these real distances are not even addressed. So if you offer the philosophical arguments of this chapter as an answer to *these* problems, you must not be surprised with the disappointment which inevitably results.

Why do people entertain hopes of closing the distances between people? There is no one answer to this question. We shall see why as the essay progresses. In what follows, I do no more than explore two sources of such hopes. First, the hopes may have an obvious moral source. Many of the distances between human beings are distances which need not exist. They are due to ignorance and prejudice. If one is morally concerned about these matters, one will want such differences lessened or, if possible, eradicated. This will be a hope to lessen or eradicate prejudice and ignorance. One may or may not admire such optimism, but this desire to close distances does not occasion the philosophical issues that I am concerned with. Nevertheless, it is one of the sources of the disappointment at a sense of the human which is compatible with serious distances between human beings.

The second source of disappointment with our conclusions that I want to discuss does lead to philosophical difficulties. In the course of this chapter we have said that our sense of the human is rooted in certain common reactions. These reactions are mixed. They are not all of the same kind. On the one hand, there are the sympathetic reactions to pain we have already mentioned. But we must remember that there is also an instinctive recoil from extreme suffering. Our reactions to the success of others are mixed: there is a gladness, but there is also envy and even anger. But, having said that, there are many reactions which are simply ruled out. We do not even consider them. We do not expect to be beaten to the ground by people with whom we pass the time of day. We do not expect a human being to react to a child who falls into his or her path, in the same way as that person would react to a stone or tin can which fell there. Of course, we have heard of the atrocities which human beings have perpetrated on each other. The protest 'That's a human being' has had no effect on such people. The agreement in reactions to which we have referred is not, therefore, a universal agreement. Nevertheless, the place it has in our lives defines the place it does not reach: it is the place we reserve for 'the monstrous'. We may say that place is below a *lower limit*, a limit to which we appeal when we say, 'That's a human being'. But this limit is not determined by some independent knowledge that we possess of what a human being is. Rather, it is our reaction, 'You can't do that!' which determines the limit, which determines the parameters of the human beyond which is the monstrous and the unthinkable.

The possibility of talking of a lower limit in this way and the agreement in reactions that it exemplifies, no matter in how rough and ready a way, may mislead us. It may lead us to think of the lower limit as the base of an agreed morality, which speaks of a far more ambitious commonality in our dealings with each other. Since this greater commonality obviously does not exist, flawed by distances between human beings, a disappointment sets in. It is a disappointment that human beings do not acknowledge each other in the way they should. This is the argument which, I believe, is based on a confusion. By looking more closely at relations between human beings, we can see how odd it is to suggest that serious distances between human beings need not exist. What we mean by human life would be radically modified, at least, if such distances did not exist. To establish these conclusions, we need to consider examples of far greater complexity than those we have considered hitherto.

In the examples we have considered, we have concentrated on

immediate expressions of and reactions to pain, anger, fear, gladness, and so on. These immediate reactions are important in the formation of such concepts. Reflection comes later. We move instinctively towards someone who doubles up in pain. We see the fear in a face as a person sees an object begin to fall in that person's direction. We see people smile when they receive good news and cry at distressing tidings. We see anger in a face as a punch is thrown, and anger in the opponent's face as retaliation occurs. These are simple examples and they were meant as a response to the sceptical attempt to drive a wedge between experiences and their natural expressions in behaviour. Nevertheless, if we concentrate exclusively on such cases, considerations which depend on cases of greater complexity will be ignored. But it is from these considerations that concerns about distances between people and our failure to acknowledge each other arise.

Consider, for example, the different reactions of people who have been abandoned by their parents when they were young. I am thinking of cases in which the child was simply unwanted. This rejection may result in deep anger in the child in later years. But what is the natural expression of this anger? It is not the kind of explosive anger which allows one to answer the question without difficulty. In this case it does more harm than good to speak of a natural expression at all in the way in which we could in the simple examples. Anger will show itself in the way in which thought of rejection enters the person's life: in thoughts about life's unfairness, in over-confidence or lack of confidence in relationships, in a desperate desire for security, and so on. Notice how the effects of the rejection often involve other people. Their responses will be no more immediate or primitive than the forms that anger takes. The reactions of others will vary widely. Among the majority who have not been rejected by their parents will be some who fail completely to appreciate the anger that such rejection can cause. There are those who show little patience with what they call worrying or lingering over the past: what's done is done and one should get on with one's life. Even among those who have been rejected, the experience may amount to very different things. For some, parenthood is a matter of the quality of the relationships; a matter of whether or not children are brought up well. Some who have been fortunate in their foster parents show little interest in discovering the identity of their parents. Others, who have not been so fortunate, may see the way in which they have been treated as an extension of the original rejection. In such cases, resentment and bitterness may go deep. For others, the desire to know their parents is not connected exclusively with the issue of the kind of parents they might have been. It is connected rather with a sense of the mystery of life, the contingencies of birth. Wanting to know the people who are responsible for bringing one into the world is part of this sense. These are simply one or two examples of different reactions to rejection. They are not, or need not, be immediately apparent in a person's life. They enter it in many different ways and these, in turn, provoke different reactions in others which are often just as subtle and difficult to discern. It is not difficult to see how this variety creates differences and distances between human beings.

Below what we called 'the lower limit', we invoked the notion of the monstrous and the unthinkable. But, as we have seen, above such a limit there are innumerable examples of what is unthinkable to some being thinkable to others. We do not invoke 'the monstrous' to account for such differences, differences which can be seen in people's loves and hates. What for some is deep love may be seen by others as over-reaction. Unconsolable grief in some may be described by others as counter-productive. When these differences occur, it is not enough to say that there are different reactions to the same love or grief. Rather, what love or grief amounts to differs for different people. The same is true in the case of our hatreds. Some people will share in the hatred of something. In other cases, we may be able to appreciate hatred that we ourselves do not have. Sometimes we may be unfortunate enough to come across a hatred and malice involving a readiness to destroy others which is beyond our comprehension. On all these matters, affinities and distances between people emerge. What kind of human life would it be if this were not the case?

It may be thought that pain is different from the examples that we have just considered, but this is not so. We are tempted to think this only if we confine ourselves to simple examples, such as the cry of pain on hitting one's thumb with a hammer. Once we consider more complex cases, the same affinities and distances that we have found elsewhere emerge. We have only to think of the differences between patients in a hospital. Sometimes, it is easy to see that someone is exaggerating about the pain that person is in. But, at other times, judgements are extremely difficult to make. Given great fortitude in one person, and a comparatively low resistance in another, do we say that they are bearing the *same* pain differently, or that they are not going through the *same* experience? We are pulled in both directions. Talk of 'fortitude' and 'low resistance' suggest some kind of comparative norm, however rough and ready. On the other hand, the fortitude and the low resistance are part of people's lives affecting, surely, what pain becomes for them when it enters their lives. In the simple cases, we said that 'I am in pain' replaces the cry of pain. Does it not follow that in the complex cases, people's dispositions can be seen as extensions – equally complex – of pain behaviour? This is most striking in cases of prolonged suffering, where the person's life *is* a life of pain, registered for others, perhaps, only by the silence and the blank look in the eyes. Confronted by such cases we may feel cut off from them despite our sympathy; cut off from a suffering beyond the reach of others.

In the complex examples that we have considered it would be impossible to deny an indeterminacy in our relations with each other. Sometimes, this is an indeterminacy *in* our judgements. We may not know whether to say that two people bear the same pain differently, or that two people are having different experiences of pain. But the main emphasis was on indeterminacy *between* people's judgements. There is no method to adjudicate between people's different judgements and reactions, differences which create distances between people and make them enigmas to each other.

Philosophers, as I have said, express disappointment at human life being like this, a disappointment which is not allayed by the assurance that human beings are not automatons. But what would human life be like without such differences? Attempts in literature to depict life without them have inevitably shown the great majority of human beings reduced to a degrading lowest common denominator. We have had examples in our time of peoples subjected to such monstrous control, manipulated by some central political authority. But in such circumstances, real and literary, we have also seen examples of the human spirit's struggles even when there was no hope of victory.

From situations such as these, a misleading and romantic message may emerge. It may be thought that what I am saying is that despite the distances between us, despite the sufferings which have ensued, it has all been worth it, a price worth paying for a genuinely human existence. Nothing could be further from my intention! I want nothing to do with the all too comfortable tones of philosophers who speak of life's adventure in circumstances such as these. In specific cases, distances between people have caused untold harm and distress. All I am saying is that it is hard to think of a human life in which such possibilities do not exist, and that a disappointment with the fact which entertains hopes of eradicating such possibilities is itself confused.

In previous chapters we have said that scepticism, at its deepest, involves denying *possibilities* of sense. In the early parts of the chapter we discussed the sceptical thesis which denied the possibility of our ever being sure of the existence of other human beings. We were asked to entertain the possibility that all other human beings are, in fact, automatons. I tried to show how such worries may exercise a hold on us. On the other hand, the anti-sceptical arguments led to a sense of disappointment. They did not seem to do justice to our sense of separation from other people. We explored the contexts in which our distances from each other are a reality. We concluded that these gave no grounds for scepticism about the sense of the human; since any sense, if romanticism is to be avoided, will include the differences and distances between human beings that we have discussed.

6

Criteria and Forms of Life

In this chapter, I want to look back at the previous five chapters. There is a way of summarizing the conclusions that we reached there which would miss what is most important concerning them. I shall first put forward a summary that it is possible to give of these chapters, and then endeavour to show what is inadequate about it; how it obscures from us the most important philosophical insights.

What we have done in the first five chapters, it may be said, is to answer a question which, despite the various contexts in which it can be asked, takes the form, 'What reason have we for saying that . . .?' For example, in chapter 1 we asked, 'What reason have we for saying that we can trust our sense-experiences?' In reply, we offered criteria for settling the matter, criteria which will tell us when conditions are favourable and when they are unfavourable. More specifically, we asked what reason we have for saying that something is the colour of an object. In reply, we offered criteria for determining the colour of something in a variety of contexts. In chapter 2, we asked what reason we have for believing that there is an external world. We offered criteria which tell us when something is 'in the mind' rather than 'really there'. More specifically, we asked how we can distinguish between perception and imagination and were given criteria by which we can tell one from the other. We did the same for the distinction between memory and imagination. In chapter 3, we returned to the distinction between primary and secondary qualities and asked whether we have any reason for saying that either give us knowledge of how things are. In reply, we offered criteria for distinguishing between appearance and reality in the two contexts. In chapter 4, we asked what reason we have for believing that we are more than a mind and its ideas, or a brain-in-a-vat, and we were offered criteria to show that we are. In chapter 5, we asked what reason we have for believing that there other human beings and that they are not automatons. We offered criteria for identifying human beings and for distinguishing between them and automatons. We asked what reason we have for saying that human beings are in pain, angry, glad, afraid, and so on. We offered criteria by which these more specific characteristics and states can be identified. We were asked how we know what people are going through in their pain and suffering, and whether we can always acknowledge or understand the anger, malice or gladness that others often display. In reply, we pointed out that in these complex contexts, criteria will have to be equally complex. They are not criteria which everyone shares; hence the differences and distances between human beings.

If we read the five chapters in this way, we shall think that what philosophy does is to provide us with *criteria for settling disputes*. Sceptics say that we *cannot* know this or that, and we reply by saying that we *can*, and proceed to produce criteria which will show that we *do* know the various things in question. But that is *not* what we were doing, and it is important to see why.

First, if we say that we are offering criteria which will settle our dispute with the sceptics, is it not odd that the criteria are so curiously ineffective? If we say to the sceptic, 'What we ordinarily say conflicts with your thesis', the trouble is that the sceptic already knows this, but is unimpressed by the fact. If we ask 'the ordinary person' to refute the sceptic, we may find that there is agreement with the sceptic on some issues and disagreement with him on others. After all, in our requests, we are asking these people to philosophize. So if our criteria amount to an appeal to what we ordinarily say, we are simply re-describing a datum which is part of the original problem. How would the fact that we still call a pillar-box red, even though it looks different under sodium lighting, solve the sceptical issue of whether we can talk about *the* colour of the pillar-box? After all, this fact, so far from solving the sceptical problem, is part of the situation which gives rise to it.

This does not mean that the appeal to criteria is unimportant. Not at all. The crucial issue concerns what that appeal amounts to. The essential difference has been expressed in this way: *the appeal to criteria is not meant to settle anything, but to elucidate what is already settled.* What we are attempting to show the sceptic is not that something is the case, where there is some chance that it is not the case. Rather, we are trying to elucidate forms of life which we share with the sceptics. What we have to show is how the sceptics' words fail to do justice to these forms of life; how they distance both themselves and us from them. In this elucidation, it is essential to show the route by which this distancing comes about. Such a 'showing' would not be the establishing of anything, but a clarifying elucidation of the forms of life we are already part of. This conclusion itself needs further clarification. This is the aim of this chapter.

The aim can be realized if we contrast the different senses of 'criteria' which take us to the heart of the problem. These different senses have been the topic of philosophical disputes in recent discussions. In what follows, I am reporting this dispute.[1]

The first notion of a criterion tells us that by noting certain characteristics under certain conditions, we can reach certain conclusions. For example, if I see someone who has been hit double-up, groan and grimace, I am going to conclude that that person is in pain. Does this mean that the sceptic has been answered? Have we now given him grounds for being certain that the person is in pain? Those who offer us this notion of criteria deny that the criteria make it certain that a person is in pain. Notice that they say that in certain circumstances these criteria work. But these circumstances do not always obtain. People pretend to be in pain when they are not. They may double up, and so on, in the way described as part of a play. Or they may be describing how they behaved when they were in pain. The implication of these possibilities is that when the criteria are present, we cannot be certain that the people are in pain. What we have is good reason to say that they are in pain. We are almost certain that they are in pain. But then the appeal to criteria is pointless, since it was supposed to give us certainty concerning the pain. As it is, it appears that the criteria fall short of contact with the pain itself.

How do the criteria manifested in a form of life differ from the first notion of criteria? Take a groan or a cry as a criterion of pain: groaning or crying out in pain. In the first notion, the circumstances not covered by the criteria are pretence, play-acting, rehearsing, and so on. But these circumstances fall within what we mean by a form of life. What this means is as follows: when a person pretends to be in pain that person is reinforcing our normal understanding of pain behaviour. Why does the person choose *this* way in which to pretend? The person's pretence is parasitic on our normal understanding. The pretence does not violate our criteria for understanding; it reinforces them. The same is true of play-acting or rehearsing the behaviour to tell another of it. Like the pretence, the play-acting and the rehearsing are parasitic on our normal understanding. When would groans or cries fall outside the form of life in which pain is understood? These would be either simple cases in which the groan turns out to be, say, a clearing of the throat, or bizarre cases of the imagination which serve to show how deep our forms of life are. The following amusing example has been used to bring out this latter point. We are told of a person in a dentist's chair undergoing treatment. Suddenly, the patient lets out a number of cries. Concerned, the dentist begins to prepare another injection of Novocain. Seeing this, the patient stops him, saying that he was not in pain, but simply calling his hamsters. The dentist is alarmed, but when he opens the door in response to his patient's request, in come the little hamsters. On other occasions, the dentist meets his patient on country walks. We, too, hear this person's cries in the lane and see the little hamsters following him. We have to admit that this is his way of calling his hamsters. But do examples such as these threaten our normal reactions to pain behaviour? Of course not.

Our reactions, our common understanding, determine the fate of this person: he is indeed the strange one.

It is because the notion of a form of life is not appreciated that the sceptic asks his question. As we have seen, the first notion of a criterion tells us what is and is not a table, or what is and is not red. This criterion tells us what is the case. It tells us whether an object in a room is or is not a table. It tells us whether the table is or is not a red table. But, then, this neglects an important feature of scepticism which we have noted; namely, that it asks how we know that a table exists when we are looking at it. It asks how we know it has a colour when we can see that it is red. The sceptic thinks his question is like, 'Is this object red?', although he gives it the form 'How do we know this object is red?' It looks as if the rebuttal of scepticism takes the form of the contradictory of the sceptic's claim. The sceptic says that the table does not exist. We reply that it does. The sceptic says that the table is not red. We reply that it is red. We put forward an alternative view. But when we elucidate a form of life, we are not asserting the existence of anything or any kind of alternative. It is a form of life within which there are assertions and denials of the existence of objects or of their colours. For us, the notion of an alternative to *that* does not arise. Our task is to show the route by which a sceptic concludes that talk of alternatives makes sense. The elucidation of a form of life, for philosophical purposes, does not show us what is the case or what is not the case. Rather, it elucidates a context within which we make our assertions and denials.

The denial of the form of life would be a denial of the human life that we share with each other. Imagine a rupture in the various common reactions that we discussed in previous chapters, the kind we can already witness in special instances. Imagine someone who laughs when in pain, groans and cries out when pleased, does not flinch when touching red-hot objects, and so on. Our common reactions, as we have said, mark such a person as the strange one, the outcast. Think of a child in whom there is no coordination between words and facial expressions. While the child says, 'I hate you', there is a smile on the child's face. Such a lack of coordination would be eerie and terrifying. Parents would feel estranged and cut off from this child. This does not mean that the child could not be the object of compassion and pity. Once again, it is our form of life, our common understanding, which identifies the terribleness of the child's condition.

At this point, further misunderstandings must be avoided. When I contrasted finding alternatives to the claim that the table is red, with finding an alternative to a form of life, I asked of the latter: What would it mean to look for an alternative to *that*? The trouble with my question is that it may give the impression of conservatism; the impression that no fundamental questions can be asked of the ways in which we live. Yet, surely, fundamental changes have taken place from time to time, so it seems as though there must be something wrong with my conclusions. Such changes, of course, must be accounted for, but as I shall show, accounting for them will simply reinforce the importance of what we have been saying about the notion of a form of life. To see this, we must do three things. First, we must say something of the ways in which these misgivings arise. Second, we must give account of genuine questions and the fundamental changes which may result from them. Third, we must discuss the way in which scepticism may try to reassert itself by seeking to extend the argument from genuine questions to questions which are bizarre and idle.

In much of what I have said in this essay in response to scepticism, I have emphasized *our* agreement in reactions, the consensus which reveals itself in the various ways in which we go on. Someone may respond to this emphasis in this way:

You have been right to emphasize the important difference between specific arguments or disagreements over whether, let us say, an object is red, and the kind of agreement in reactions in which the meaning of 'red' is rooted. Without this latter agreement, we have insisted, we could give no account of specific instances of agreement or disagreement. But the agreement in reactions is *our* agreement, an agreement between human beings. This makes it look as if the determination of the distinction between the real and the unreal is an anthropocentric affair. It depends on ways in which we happen to think. But, surely, the distinction between appearance and reality is independent of whatever we care to say or think.

If our conception of the real is simply *our* conception, how do we ever know whether *our* conception corresponds to reality *as it really is*. And if whatever conception we have is *our* conception, it seems that we can *never* have contact with reality as it really is.

Here the sceptical challenge seems to reassert itself with renewed vigour.

The first thing to be said about this sceptical challenge is that it ignores an extremely important feature of the agreement in reactions which I emphasized; namely, the fact that we do not *make* an agreement to react in this way. The agreement shows itself in our reactions. The sceptical objections make it look as though we stood outside these agreements, deciding whether to make them or not. Given that picture, it does look as if we decide what is real or unreal. But I do not decide whether the table is red. I have to look to find out. Neither do I decide to react in the ways I find others react too, the ways which fix what we mean by the word 'red'. Consider the following helpful example. In order to promote itself, a fashion house may give specific names to various shades of colour, names with which it hopes it will become associated. Here, as a matter of policy, it set up a convention with regard to colours. We can give the dates on which this convention is established and outline the purpose it serves. But we cannot do this with our agreements about colours. The convention of the fashion house is, in fact, dependent on this agreement. They did not set up a convention to determine the meaning of 'red', 'green', and so on. On the contrary, they took these colours for granted in setting up their convention. They did not take them for granted because of any policy decision or because they decided to. They had no choice in the matter. The accusation that the conclusions that we have reached make the distinction between the real and the unreal a matter of choice is unfounded. Furthermore, in this connection, it is important to remember what we said about the *active* self in chapters 3 and 4, a self not set apart, not a passive recipient of sensory-experiences, but a self active *in* the world.

Again, consider the example of mathematics. We agree in our reactions concerning what going on in the same way amounts to in the series, 2, 4, 6, 8, 10. . . . Without this agreement, there would be no mathematics. But, again, this does not mean that mathematics is at our disposal. It is not open to us to change the numbers in a calculation in order to bring about a more desirable result. Mathematics is not open to our manipulations. If questions were asked about why we call this 'red' or why we call this 'counting', we might be able to give an account of why it is natural to proceed as we do, but this would not be to give a more fundamental justification of our agreement in reactions. On the contrary, our questions, in this context, take our agreement in reactions for granted.

At this stage, we must turn to the second point that we have to discuss; namely, the context in which questions are appropriate rather than inappropriate. These questions often lead to fundamental changes in the ways in which we proceed. As we shall see, the danger here is of running different examples together, examples which require very different discussions.

At this point, I want to concentrate on our knowledge of the empirical world. It is important to recognize that so far from undermining our agreement in reactions, critical questioning may be a feature of some contexts where those reactions are found. The example of scientific enquiry comes to mind. Here, critical questioning and testing is the essence of the investigation. But this does not mean that there is not a great deal that we take for granted in such contexts. If, after conducting the appropriate experiment, we asked a scientist why the absence of certain results should show that a certain hypothesis has not been proved, he would be extremely puzzled. Experiential testing is what he means by showing whether a hypothesis has or has not been established. He can no more change the data to bring about a desirable result than the mathematician can change the numbers in a calculation at his convenience. But, of course, it is also true that, given the unhelpful results in an experiment, one scientist may settle for them, whereas another asks further imaginative questions which change the terms of reference in such a way that it brings about a fundamental change in the context of experimentation; it changes the parameters of what was taken for granted. But such changes as these do not undermine what has been said about forms of life. They may appear to do so only if we forget the *scientific* context in which these questions arise. It is not as if new scientific paradigms are plucked from the air, no matter how revolutionary the scientific changes may be. This is why it is possible to write a *history* of science, the history of a developing science. I am not ignoring the fact that some scientists have gone to their graves refusing to contemplate new directions that science takes. They have often felt that new procedures lack the elegance of older ones, or that the new interests being pursued are less important than others and that the pursuit of them constitutes a loss of seriousness in the subject. Even so, without a scientific background, even such fundamental disputes as these would be meaningless. They reinforce rather than undermine the notion of a form of life.

To illustrate this, we need to turn to our third point, the way in which, from a proper recognition of the place of critical questioning, we can be led to ask sceptical questions which obscure completely the conclusions that we have endeavoured to reach. First, because of the kind of revisions of conclusions that we find in scientific investigation, it may be said that we never know what reality is like. If we can be mistaken once, we can be mistaken again. How do we ever know that we are not in fact mistaken when we think we are certain about our conclusions? Here, the sceptical question has taken flight from the actual contexts in which scientific revisions are made. On such a view, the reasons for such revisions become a complete mystery. To begin with, this ignores the fact that when scientific discoveries are made, this does not mean that what was held previously was always totally false. It may be that some explanatory hypothesis has a more restricted application than was hitherto thought to be the case. The restricting of its sphere of application is itself shown by experimentation which may not have been possible at an earlier date in that science, perhaps for technical reasons, or because the imaginative leaps necessary to see the necessity for such experiments had not taken place. In any case, what we have here is a case of *building* on past achievements rather than destroying them.

But, on the sceptic's view, since we cannot have knowledge of reality, we cannot speak of either advance or regress in science.

In order for the sceptic's case to seem credible, it must be *general* in its application, but trade on *specific* instances, so that it appears to have practical import. For example, by the use of microscopes we find out something about physical surfaces, or the constitution of the blood, which we did not know otherwise. Here, we can speak of something being the case which we did not know. But, then, the sceptic generalizes and postulates a something we can never know, no matter how much we experiment, a 'something we know not what'. At this point, we have abstracted the doubt from all practical contexts. In the latter, as we have seen, we deal with the results of experimentation and the revisions of them which further experimentation may necessitate. Here, we do not speak in terms of absolutes as the sceptic does – absolute ignorance or absolute knowledge. Nothing that we mention could satisfy the sceptic, since any experiential result that we mention is attributed to a 'something' which further experiments may show is other than we take it to be. It follows that this 'something' can have no nature or fall under any description, since any actual description we offer will be, on the sceptic's arguments, revisable. So no human endeavour takes us any nearer to the nature of this 'something'. It is forever beyond the reach of humans. Little wonder that some have said that knowledge of it is reserved for God and angels. Such scepticism constitutes a denial of the human. In this particular case, it obscures from us the actual things we come to know through scientific investigation. In fact, such scepticism can give no account of the notion of investigation.

But worse is to follow. If, in fact, the result of any experiment is open to revision and this process is endless, *no revision can be ruled out in principle*. And if that is so, what right do we have to be certain about anything? Even that which we do not question is open to revision in principle. After all, who would have ever thought that human beings would fly? Once we say this, it seems that our familiar surroundings can only be taken for granted by us in some conditional way, perhaps for pragmatic reasons. Perhaps it is all illusion, perhaps it is all a dream, but, since we are getting on reasonably well with what we have, we will settle for it. This terrifying picture of the precariousness of our world is the end-point of scepticism. Those who entertain it may view with a knowing detachment the comic condition of human beings as they take for granted that which they have no reason to be certain of.

If no outcome of further discovery can be ruled out in principle, how do we know that what we take to be the most permanent of objects in our world may not be at risk? How do we know that the chairs we sit on, or the tables we sit at, will not simply vanish? How do we know that they do not vanish as soon as we stop looking at them, coming back into existence at the very moment we resume our gaze? How do we know that houses will not suddenly change into flowers or evaporate? How do we know that cows and pigs will not start to conduct discussions and write poetry? Indeed, how do we know that they do not do so already? I once saw an amusing cartoon in which cows in a field, seeing tourists approach, give up their learned discussions and say, 'Here come the tourists, we'd better get back to chewing the cud'. Perhaps cows only graze for our benefit.

What are we to say in face of these projections which are meant to make us sceptical of our familiar surroundings? One reaction which we have already met is to try to combat these suggestions as though they were contradictions of claims we are making.[2] Thus, in response to the claim that books may suddenly vanish, we retort that we have good reasons – criteria – for saying that books do not suddenly vanish. A philosopher may appeal to the fact that he has read millions of printed words on many thousands of printed pages, without encountering a single instance of a printed word vanishing from a page, or being replaced by another printed word suddenly without an external cause. He may appeal to the fact that this is not an isolated experience on his part. It is one which is shared by everyone. Thus we have, on this basis, overwhelming evidence to say that books and the words printed in them do not simply vanish. This evidence is just as conclusive, the philosopher concludes, as the evidence that houses do not turn into flowers. Perhaps he would have said that there is equally good evidence to support the view that cows and pigs do not write poetry. Of course, they may do so in children's books, but we know how to respond to such stories. No one has come across a poetry-writing pig in real life, so we have excellent grounds for concluding that pigs do not write poetry. The sceptic may say that houses may turn into flowers or pigs may write poetry, but we have conclusive evidence that this is impossible.

The attempted rebuttal of scepticism here relies on producing counter-evidence to what seems to be a specific factual claim. This is the confusion that the rebuttal falls into. The searching for good evidence to show that houses do not turn into flowers, or to show that pigs do not write poetry, seems as hysterical as the suggestion that this might be the case. It takes us back to the distinction between the two kinds of criteria with which we began this chapter: criteria which determine what is and what is not the case, and criteria which manifest themselves in our forms of life. The rebuttal makes it look as if checking that words on the printed page do not vanish or come and go, some words suddenly replacing others, is on a par with checking a book to see if any pages are missing. After an annoying number of occasions on which one has bought a book only to find some pages missing (especially in books at reduced prices), one may be careful thereafter to check any further books one buys in such circumstances. One has good evidence that pages are missing from some books and one's cautious checking thereafter makes sense in that light. But what would we make of someone who, when asked what he was up to in thumbing through a book, replied, 'I'm just checking that words do not vanish suddenly from the page'? What would we make of such a person's words? We might think it was the first sign of madness. Such a person would certainly not be produced as evidence of commendable caution. And what of the person we find lurking in the hedgerows hoping to catch the cows composing poetry? The aping of those patient cameramen who record the nocturnal behaviour of animals only serves to underline the madness. The person is not even in the category of our strange eccentric whose cries, as if in pain, cause hamsters to follow the caller down country lanes.

The point of these extravagant examples is to show that we do not know what to make of the suggestions put to us. We cannot do anything with them. So if we say in reply to the sceptic that we do not verify that houses do not turn into flowers; do not verify that words do not vanish suddenly from the pages of books to be replaced by other words; or do not verify that cows do not write poetry, we are not making any kind of apology. It is not that such matters should be verified, but we have not got round to doing so. It would be a sign of madness if someone were to set out to verify these matters. We are saying that the sceptic's words have no purchase. They do not have a use. We would not and should not respond to the sceptical projections by saying, 'We can assure you that houses, printed pages and cows do not behave in the way you describe'. Such an assurance would obscure from us the way in which our common understanding in our forms of life rules out the sceptic's suggestions. It would be to underestimate and mischaracterize the ways in which forms of life go deep with us. This depth may be illustrated by a joke, which I particularly like, which illustrates the limits of humour. To understand the philosophical application of the joke is to understand the difference between the two senses of criteria that we have been discussing: those criteria which determine what is and what is not the case, and those criteria which reveal the conceptual parameters of our forms of life. A soldier is asked, 'If you saw a battleship approaching the position you are guarding in the middle of the desert, what would you do?' The soldier replies, 'I'd sink it with my torpedo'. The instructor asks, 'Where did you get that torpedo from?' The soldier replies, 'The same place from which you got your battleship'.

Before concluding this chapter, a word must be said about questioning criteria in a way that is different from those we have discussed. I have in mind, now, not the critical questions which are characteristic of the activity within which the questions arise, as is the case in scientific investigation, nor the bizarre attempts at projections which ask us how we know that houses do not turn into flowers or that cows do not write poetry. Rather, I have in mind questions which challenge and upset our previous ways of carrying on. These are not questions to which we can reply, 'This is how we do carry on', because to heed them is not to carry on in that way any longer. The voice to which we have to pay attention is an accusing voice, which reveals the folly of our ways. How, if at all, does the way we have discussed agreement in reactions in this chapter, or the notion of forms of life, allow for questions such as these? It may be claimed that such questions are the essence of what we mean by education, where, through reflective criticism, a culture is brought to confront itself.

I think we must tread warily in this context. We have already mentioned critical questions which are characteristic of the activity in which they occur. There are also questions which are the voice, not of an accuser, but of a tempter: 'Why should I tell the truth when it would pay me to lie?' Such a question is recognized as a temptation and, in that sense, falls within the parameters of the moral although it may seem to question it. But we still have the accuser's questions, questions which may ask me whether I should love what I love, or fear what I fear. These questions are sceptical about my love and fear. What has philosophy to say about them? How far will our emphasis on agreed or shared reactions take us in this context?

Some philosophers would like to say that our agreed reactions in our forms of life take us a considerable distance in understanding the questions of the accuser, questions which are meant to disturb these forms of life. Here, too, there are limits – serious limits – to what can be questioned or denied. We may or may not be angry at a particular offence, but what would it mean to speak of being angry at a speck of dust? We may or may not be afraid of impending danger, but what would it mean to be afraid of a pin? Some special context may give this sense: the pin may be the pin in a grenade. So although anger and fear may be expressed in relation to very different matters, this variety occurs within the parameters of what is recognizably human.

How far does such an argument take us when considering fundamental challenges to a form of life? At the end of the last chapter, we discussed how one human being may be an enigma to another. Common reactions do not mean reactions shared by everyone – not in the contexts we are discussing now. There is a danger of arguing in the following way: there are conceptual limits to what we can be said to be afraid of or angry about, since differences belong to human life and occur within limits. In acknowledging this, it may be argued, we are acknowledging a life in which we all share, acknowledging a sense of community. When we are asked critical questions of how we live, these questions are themselves a request for seriousness, a plea to be taken seriously. In acknowledging the questions in this way, we are restoring a sense of community, the sense of a shared life. I think this form of argument is confused. We must now see why.[3]

At the end of the last chapter, I spoke of the indeterminacy which is often found in our relations with each other. I think we need to remind ourselves of it again here. Often the disagreements between us will take the form of wondering what we should be afraid of, or what we should love, where criteria recognized by all involved will settle the matter for us. I may think that I have reason to be afraid of someone because he can outbid me, and effectively put me out of business. But I am mistaken. My fear turns out to be misplaced. The person I feared does not have the money and I become the victim of another whom I did not fear, but who had the money. Here, there is no change in my *conception* of fear. I simply feared the wrong person through ignorance of the facts. Again, I may think I loved someone, but later come to see that I was simply infatuated. So between the time when I thought I loved her and the time when I came to see that I did not, there is no change in my conception of love. But, at the other times, I may say, 'I thought I knew what love was, but I didn't'. Here, there is a change in my conception of love. When I refer to my former state, I am not referring to a mistake within a conception of love. I am calling that conception a mistake. I do not mean by 'mistake' here anything like an accusation of sentimentality or romanticism. Rather, I am thinking of seeing possibilities as *possibilities of love* which I did not possess or understand before. What I came to may or may not be appreciated by others. Some may see the kind of love that I have acquired and still be unable to, or may not want to, give themselves to it. Others may simply not understand what I am talking about. Instead of characterizing such differences as failure to acknowledge what is human, I would say that it is these differences which are characteristic of life among humans. If we could understand these different conceptions of love, no doubt we would find that all of them avoid the absurdities that there would be in loving a saucer of mud. Yet, that fact would in no way prevent the differences and distances between people to which I am drawing attention. The presence of critical questions may be part of the direction in which a person's allegiances are moving, signs that a perspective is beginning to lose its hold.

There is a danger of thinking that critical questions are *always* appropriate. Not to acknowledge them then becomes inappropriate in itself; a denial of a sense of the human. But we cannot say, in the abstract, that critical questions are appropriate or that it is good to ask them. In relation to fear, think of the question of why we should fear God. It may be said, with good reason, that the only worthwhile faith is a reflective faith (which is *not* to say an intellectual one). This will apply to reflection on the kind of fear that fear of God is. Do we fear a policeman in the sky? But let us suppose that the fear of God does not take this form; that the fear is not cringing or servile. What if then someone asks, 'Why fear God?' It is tempting to assume that intellectual rectitude demands that the question should be asked. But it may be characteristic of such faith that asking the question is itself the first sign of rebellion against it. Compare with asking why one should respect one's parents. That is not asking whether one's parents deserve respect for something or other: it is asking whether the fact that they are one's parents should be connected with any kind of respect. It is this *conception* of respect which is being questioned. In questioning religion, too, a certain *kind* of fear is being questioned. That is why it has been said that to submit God to moral judgement is to kill him in one's own heart. Some will ask the question, while others reject it. No doubt it can be shown that the tradition from which the question is asked, and the tradition which rejects it, have conceptions of fear which do not fall into the kind of unintelligibility that we find in someone who says they are afraid of a speck of dust. But that would do nothing to remove or lessen the differences between those who are prepared and those who are not prepared to ask why we should fear God.

How are these discussions and distances between people related to the two senses of criteria that we have discussed? Clearly, the fundamental differences that I am talking about are not differences within an agreed conception of love or fear. Rather, as we have seen, the distances are between *different conceptions* of love and fear. Are we to say that these different conceptions exist within *the same* form of life? We can say that to imagine them is to imagine them *in a form of life*. What saying this means, however, is that the *various* ways in which we live show the parameters within which we seriously talk of love and hate. Bizarre, unintelligible cases are ruled out. But this leaves untouched, as we saw at the end of the last chapter, the *various* ways in which love and hate are taken up in people's lives. It may be said that to imagine love and hate in a form of life *is* to imagine the differences, not only *in* loves and hates where common criteria of what is at stake can be found, but between *different conceptions* of love and hate which create distances between us. It is not the task of philosophy to arbitrate between these conceptions (a confused conception of arbitration), but to be as faithful as it can to the form of life in which they clash, co-operate, criticize, or simply pass each other by.

7

Moral Possibilities

In the course of this essay we have paid considerable attention to the notion of the self in various contexts: the self which is said to know that such-and-such is the case; the self which is at the centre of the distinction between what is objectively real and what is in the mind; the self which stands in various relations to other human beings. In this connection we have discussed the constant threat of scepticism: the scepticism which questions the possibility of our knowing anything; the scepticism which questions whether any individual can be certain that there are other human beings. We have asked whether these sceptical doubts can be answered by criteria of verification which will tell us what is the case. Such criteria would yield results which contradict the sceptic's claims. When the sceptic denies that we know that there are human beings, such criteria enable us to reply that we *do* know that there are human beings. We have cast doubt on the claim that scepticism can be refuted in this way. Instead, we have concentrated on the criteria which show themselves in a form of life. In doing so, we are not trying to settle anything, but to elucidate the importance of what is already settled in the human life that we share with each other.

We cannot get very far in discussing the self and its relations to other human beings without bringing in moral questions. After all, relations between human beings are often constituted or criticized in terms of moral considerations. But scepticism questions what these considerations come to. The question it raises, at its deepest, concerns *the possibility of morality*. The sceptic suggests that it cannot be what it claims to be. There are many different ways in which the sceptical challenge may be presented. What follows is simply one attempt at opening up discussion of some central issues.

In my relations with other human beings I may be told that I must be truthful, kind and considerate. Suppose that I ask, 'Why?' What answer could I be given? Two answers have dominated the history of moral philosophy. According to the first, I must be given good reasons to conduct myself in this way in relation to my fellow human beings. This seems eminently reasonable, since to refuse to give me any reasons is to refuse to show me the point of acting in this way. Why should I do what is pointless? It seems that there is no alternative to providing such reasons. But this is where the sting of scepticism is felt. Once the reasons are made explicit, it is argued, morality is exposed as nothing more than enlightened self-interest. Morality is shown to be other than it claims to be. Ordinarily, we contrast morality and self-interest, but morality turns out to be just one form of it. It is because of this conclusion that a second, very different, answer is offered to the question of why we should heed moral considerations. The trouble with the first answer, it is said, is that it makes moral obligation a hypothetical matter. On that view, we should act in a certain way because it leads to certain results. But since such results are always contingent, moral obligation seems devoid of any necessity. Yet this does not seem to satisfy what is claimed for morality. If we say that we do not want to play better tennis, in the end, that is our affair. But suppose we had told someone a despicable lie and someone remonstrates with us about what we have done. Would it be any kind of defence to say, 'Well, I don't want to tell the truth or stop behaving in this way'? Of course not. We would be told, 'But you *ought*. You *must*'. It is this 'ought', this 'must', which cannot be accounted for by the first answer too. What does the notion of necessity involved in it amount to? No intelligible account can be given of it. It seems as if we are relying on the 'must' to have some kind of magic effect on the person we are trying to convince. And so we are faced with an unpromising choice, it seems: either we give reasons for heeding moral considerations, only to find that these reasons expose morality's real nature, or we refuse to give reasons, leaving us with a language which tells us what we *must* do, but which harbours an unintelligible, magical conception of necessity. In either case, we come to a sceptical conclusion: morality cannot possibly be what it claims to be.

Let us look in more detail at the first answer. How is it arrived at? If you tell me that I must help someone in distress, you obviously want me to heed your command. But why should I do so? There would be little point in my being told that I should act in this way because you want me to. Why should I pay any attention to what *you* want? If you want to move me to act in a certain way, you will have to find something which will interest *me*. The appeal must be to my self-interest. The point is not merely a psychological one. It is presented as though it were *logically* compelling. If you want me to act kindly towards someone, you must get *me* to want to so do. The action, if it is to be *mine* in any real sense, must be based on my wants. This, of course, is not only true of me, but of anyone. We must be shown why it pays to be good.

According to the first view that we are considering, there is no difficulty about showing that morality pays. What is morality except a set of rules to regulate the behaviour of self-interested individuals? If I could manipulate fellow human beings in any way I wanted, or beat them into reliable submission, there would be no necessity for me to pay any attention to moral considerations. But, of course, the world is not like that. It does not obey our every whim. We are dependent on others, as they are on us. We need each other if we are going to get through this difficult world. Morality is the means by which we do so. In this way, morality is shown to be the rational product of the clash of self-interested individuals.[1]

On this view, I am given good reasons why I should pay attention to the virtues. We need to equip ourselves with them in order to prosper in this life. Of course, not every virtuous person does prosper, and on given occasions most people do not prosper. Nevertheless, this does not mean that they have no reason to be just, because *on the whole* it pays to be so. We do not desert a policy which is generally beneficial because it is not beneficial in specific instances. General benefit outweighs occasional disadvantages. Of course life can be cruel and, for some, there are only occasional advantages and a general disadvantage. Even in these cases, it is argued, the individual *had* good reason to heed moral considerations. The odds were on that side; they always are.

What are we to make of this argument? As we have already said, the first reaction that one has is that it violates our common understanding of the demands that morality makes on us. Instead of moral considerations overriding self-interest, these are made a function of it! And when we turn to look for the implications of such a view in specific cases, the vulgarization involved in it becomes all to evident. Consider the cases of generosity and friendship. In terms of the analysis that we are considering, generosity and friendship become a 'higher' form of prudence. On this view, there is not to be a spontaneous grabbing of what one wants. Rather, one has to take a longer-term view of prudence and put the immediate satisfaction of self-interest aside. By so doing, while losing in the short term, it leads to long-term advantage. It pays to be generous to another, since although it may be in one's interest to do ill by the other *now*, one's own fortunes may change in the future and one will need the help of others. Since such sudden changes of fortune are characteristic of life, generosity turns out to be the best long-term policy. Likewise, it pays to befriend another, for who knows when one will need a friend oneself? But generosity and friendship are not *for* anything. Of course, there is no difficulty in coming up with examples in which the analysis offered is a faithful portrayal of what generosity and friendship come to in these cases. But these cases are those we recognize as *perversions* of generosity and friendship. The irony is that we are offered the perversions as the analysis of generosity and friendship.

When we take the analysis further, the picture becomes a darker one. What we are offered seems to fly in the face of common experience. It is hard to argue that in terms of self-interest there is a happy marriage between decency and worldly success. Has not the cry rung down the ages, 'Why do the wicked prosper?' The analysis that we are considering responds by saying that such protest is misplaced. If only decent people calculated properly they would find that the wicked had not prospered at all since, as life shows, decency always comes out on top, since it pays to be good! Do we know what to do with a response of this kind? It may be said that, tenuous though the hold of moral considerations may be on us from time to time, even at moments such as these, we would recognize that what we succumb to in our selfishness certainly cannot be offered as an account of the moral considerations that we ignore in doing so. When that is not true, and a more empirical attitude prevails, it may be said by one who cares little for what ought to be done, that under the skin, the other 'decent' ones are all the same. It is just that they have enjoyed better luck than the cynic. I do not mean by this contrast that decency amounts to saying that one is better than others are, but that the cynic denies that the struggle to be decent amounts to anything worthwhile. The picture darkens because the voice of the cynic at our side comes with an insidious whisper, 'We know what's it really all about, don't we? Love, friendship, loyalty, generosity – it all comes down to looking after Number One when you think about it'. As we have seen, when some philosophers think about it, they seem to agree.

It may be said that in the attack on the analysis that we have been offered, it has been assumed that every decent act must pay and that everyone who tries to be decent prospers in the way envisaged. What was actually said is that in *general* this is the case. The odds are on the side of our needing the virtues in this life. The analysis, therefore, allows for those occasions on which the wicked prosper. It is not so blatantly ignorant of the ways of the world as its critics would have us believe.

Accommodating these modifications on behalf of the analysis, so far from rescuing it, plunges it into further incoherencies. Consider the concession that, on a given occasion, it may not pay to be good. Great personal sacrifice may be asked of one.

According to the argument, the reason why the great sacrifice must be paid is that, in the long term, it will turn out to be worth it. Sacrifice now, live later. What is absolutely clear, on such a view, is that no account can be given of anyone who dies for the sake of his friends: it becomes a mystery why people have allowed themselves to be tortured to death rather than bring about the death of friends by revealing their whereabouts. Death cannot be something which will be accommodated in terms of the game the analysis asks us to play. If the point of being good is to serve my self-interest, the certainty of death must always rob goodness of its point. There is no use in saying that I *had* reason to be just when setting out on life's journey because the odds are that we need the virtues in this life. If I am confronted by the certainty of my death as a result of the virtuous policy, surely all bets are off. I do not need the odds to tell me that the certainty of my death renders pointless the game I have been asked to play. In terms of the analysis, heroism becomes the height of folly, a pointless act. Once again, the analysis flies in the face of a common understanding.

The same is true when we consider another modification of the analysis. As we have seen, it is claimed that our needing the virtues is a matter of probability. It is not inconceivable therefore, given that it is a matter of the odds, for someone to cheat them. Think, then, of someone in whom gambling instincts developed early. The idea that lying, cheating and betraying could pay off seemed attractive. And so it turned out. At the end of life, we find this person looking back with relish on the achievements. 'What a lucky day for me when I gambled against the odds on my vices paying off if I was shrewd enough.' The absence of any remorse at the end would normally count as an additional indictment of such a person. But the analysis we are offered is silent when confronted by this scene. There is no point in saying to such a person, 'Think of the odds at the outset. You had good reason to be virtuous'. What effect can the appeal to such odds have on this person now looking back at a life well spent? Of course, from a moral point of view the life has been ill spent. The analysis leads to a denial of the possibility of this moral response.

According to the view that we are considering, moral considerations, as we have seen, are a function of our interdependence as human beings. This is an inter-dependence that we cannot escape, and if we try to we shall soon be found out and pay the penalty. So the argument runs. We have already countered it by pointing out that some have escaped this so-called inescapable interdependence without paying the penalty. The incredible fact is that the analysis, while thinking that such an escape is impossible, actually concedes that if it were possible, all reasons for heeding moral considerations would evaporate. We are told that if others could be manipulated or beaten into reliable submission like donkeys, there would be no reason to pay attention to the virtues. But is not this precisely what tyrants and dictators throughout the ages have succeeded in doing? We are all too familiar with pictures and accounts of the atrocities perpetrated on their victims. In saying that we have nothing to say to such villains, the analysis that we are offered once again flies in the face of our common understanding.

What, then, are we to do in face of these unfortunate results, results which equate morality and self-interest and which leave us with nothing to say in face of unspeakable atrocities, devoid of any resources from which to condemn their perpetrators? Do we not want to say in face of the selfish response to moral obligations, 'I don't want to', 'No matter, you *must*'? So far from being rendered speechless by the atrocities of tyrants, do we not want to say that such evil *must not* be tolerated? Morality is not a function of enlightened self-interest. Rather, it introduces a different mode of discrimination into human life. It is not content to be told that we want such-and-such. It asks whether we *should* want such things. Given that there is no moral objection to what we seek, it does not follow that it can be pursued by any and every means. How we go about getting what we want is brought under the same moral scrutiny as what we want. This shows that the relation between means and ends cannot, of itself, throw much light on moral considerations, since means and ends both have to come under moral scrutiny.

Notice, that we say that they *have* to come under such scrutiny. There is a necessity here, captured by the moral 'must'. Morality, it is said, is not a matter of desire, the fatal flaw in the first view, but a matter of duty. The main characteristic of moral duty is that it overrides our desires. Here we have arrived at our second view, one which claims to provide us with both the nature and motivation of moral action. The nature of moral obligation is its overridingness. The moral 'ought' overrides all other 'oughts'. It does so in the name of duty. A moral action is one done from a sense of a duty which overrides all other considerations.[2]

As we shall see, the trouble with the second view is that, like the first view, it seems to fly in the face of our common understanding once we elucidate further what is involved in this notion of moral duty and the overriding character that it is supposed to possess.

It is not hard to see the kind of situation that the appeal to duty is meant to address. If I tell someone that he ought to take an umbrella with him, it is usually because I think it is going to rain and I assume that the person does not want to get wet. If I tell someone that this is the right train to catch, I am assuming that he or she wants to get to where that train is going. But suppose that I find out that the person I am talking to does not want what I thought was wanted. Despite getting wet, the person enjoys it, singing and dancing in the rain. In that case, to insist that the person must take an umbrella denigrates into an interference which has no justification. It may also turn out that the person does not want to go where the train is going. It would be absurd to say that despite this fact the train is still the right train and that it ought to be travelled on. Examples such as these are said to exhibit hypothetical imperatives. A person is told that he ought to do something if he wants such-and-such. If it turns out that he does not want it, the 'ought' promptly loses the support it needs in order for it to have a point.

By contrast, the moral 'ought' is said to be a categorical and not an hypothetical imperative. If a person is told that he must not tell a despicable lie, and the reply is that he does not want to heed this advice, the moral 'ought' does not retreat, pointless, defeated, in face of this declared desire. On the contrary, it reasserts itself by retorting, 'Well, you *ought* to'. The moral demand is categorical and it overrides our desires. Moral demands should not be at the mercy of our inclination. Our moral obligations cannot be made to depend on the capricious fact of whether we feel inclined to fulfil them on any occasion.

It has to be pointed out that according to the second view that we are considering, the rejection of inclination as having anything to do with morality is meant to include anything which may be called moral inclinations, not simply those self-interested inclinations which so obviously clash with moral obligations on many occasions. What is this reference to moral inclinations meant to include? First, the view is meant to include those who are inclined to act morally, but from the wrong motives. Consider the cases of grocers, butchers and others who always give their customers the correct change. They never cheat them. They fulfil their duty in this respect towards them. But more is needed, since it may turn out that although a grocer never has any inclination to give anything other than the correct change, this is because he believes that if he did so, it would soon get known, and this would affect his business adversely. He concludes, therefore, that duty is the best policy. But although his actions *conform* to what moral duty requires, they are not done out of respect for that duty. A moral action must not simply accord with that duty, it must be done out of respect for it as well. That respect, it is claimed, has nothing to do with our inclinations.

This conclusion may strike us as premature. So far, we have emphasized selfish inclinations which clash with what morality requires and inclinations to abide by moral requirements from the wrong motives. But what of moral inclinations such as generosity, kindness, compassion, pity, and so on? Surely their moral significance cannot be denied. The second view that we are considering tries not to ignore them, but assigns a place to them which is highly unsatisfactory. A consequence could be attributed to the second view which it rightly denies having to embrace. It may be thought that on the view we are considering, the very presence of generous or compassionate inclinations in a person while performing an action rules out the possibility of the action being a moral act. Such a thesis appears to be grotesque. It would involve saying that if money is given to charity by someone who has been moved to pity by the sight of starving children, the action is morally worthless. There need be no such implication in the second view. What it does say, however, is that if we want to know what is of moral worth in the action, that worth will turn out to have nothing to do with the presence of those inclinations. It may be conceded that these inclinations play an invaluable role in nurturing our moral duties. Their presence in an individual makes it more likely that that person will fulfil moral duties. Inclinations are thus aids to moral endeavour. We have a duty to cultivate them for that reason, but they are not, in themselves, relevant to the essence of our moral actions.

This answer will not do. Like the others we have considered, it flies in the face of our common understanding. A person may give money to charity because it is a moral duty to do so. But that person may regret the absence from his or her behaviour of that compassion in which another pities the starving. This absence of compassion may be regarded by the person as a *moral* failing. The second view can make no sense of this. But clearly there are cases in which acting from a sense of duty may be regarded as very much a second-best to the actions which flow directly from moral inclinations. Consider the case of a father absorbed in play with his children. Another father, unable to achieve this, regards it as a failure, a shortcoming in himself. It is not that he does not care about his children. He does. He plays dutifully with them for a period of every day when many do not. But he is never absorbed in them. He sees in such absorption a kind of self-forgetting which is not in him. The point at issue for the second view is not whether it agrees with this moral criticism. The point is that its parameters do not allow it to be recognized as a possible moral criticism. It is at this point that it obscures our common understanding. The inclinations are themselves of moral significance in these contexts. Indeed, it is the morally striking thing about them, and this is what the second view cannot accommodate.

Why should this be so? There are two considerations which may be at work in the second view. Because of the kind of examples of moral inclinations that we have just considered, we may make the mistake of thinking that *these* express the essence of moral action. It then appears that if these inclinations are not present, no moral obligations remain. Defenders of the second view argue that in this way the necessity of moral demands is threatened. What if, as nature would have it, a person has not been bestowed with a compassionate nature? Does it follow that such a person has no obligations towards the needy who may be in his care? Surely it will not do to respond if told to look after them, 'I would but I am not of a compassionate disposition'. The reply would be, 'You *must* look after them'. It is the need for this kind of reminder which often gives credence to the second view. But there is a confusion in the use that is made of it. Others may say to us, or we may say to ourselves, that we *must* help. We are reminding ourselves of an obligation where there is some danger of our neglecting it. It is this danger which gives the reminder its point. We are called back to something. In ideal circumstances, such a reminder is unnecessary. Therefore, from the fact that we often need to be reminded of our duty to help, it does not follow that if we help without such a reminder, we always do so from a sense of duty. It is simply a confusion to assume that the language which a reminder makes necessary would also be the appropriate language if no such reminder were necessary. In any case, it is not an all-or-nothing affair. The fact that someone does not react with a spontaneous compassion for the plight of others does not mean that when help is given, after a reminder of the duty to help, the action is devoid of moral worth.

A second, related consideration is this: when someone tries to get me to do something I do not want to do, it may not be realized that it is a moral matter for me, a matter of principle. I may clarify the situation by saying, 'It's my moral duty. I just can't do that'. Such a remark simply shows that moral considerations are involved. It does not follow from saying this that my motive in acting or refraining to act is duty.

What we are finding in the discussion of our two views is that neither of them will fit all of the cases. Some philosophers spend a great deal of time trying to rescue one or other of the two views from the inevitable counter-examples paraded against them.[3] The views become modified to such an extent that they are barely recognizable by the end of the exercise. I am going to make a very different proposal. Surely, as far as philosophy is concerned, our task is to clarify the nature of different moral possibilities and the various relations in which they may stand to one another. Given that the two views that we have considered do not do justice to all cases, we must resist the temptation of thinking that our task is to find a third view which will accommodate them all. What we need to recognize is that there is no all-embracing moral theory, and that those which we have are blown-up generalisations of certain aspects of our moral experience. Once we give up the search for such a theory we can at least endeavour to give the variety of moral possibilities the kind of attention it deserves. If we do not do this and try instead to find a definition of moral action, no sooner will we do so than someone will think of an example of an action which may be called 'good' but which falls outside the definition.

These conclusions hold for general attempts to define the meaning of a moral 'ought'. For example, in an effort to do justice to the overriding nature of the moral claim, it may be said that the moral 'ought' overrides an ought of any other kind.[4] But if this definition is applied to every action without any discrimination, the results become far-fetched. We do not have to think of a clash between an important aesthetic consideration and a moral consideration to bring out this point. It can be made in terms of a clash between a clear moral obligation and a piece of unadorned self-indulgence. Let us suppose that on a certain day of the week, I visit my invalid mother. If I miss a visit she is very upset. I am in no doubt that I have a moral obligation to visit her. On one particular week, I am informed that I am the winner of thousands of pounds in a sweepstake. A condition of being given the prize is that I must collect it in person on a given day. No excuses are acceptable. That is part of the luck of the draw. The day in question turns out to be the very one on which I am supposed to visit my mother. We do not want to change the example by suggesting that the person would use his prize money to finance good deeds including good deeds to his mother. No, he is going to use the money to have a good time, spending it on things which give him pleasure. So what we have is a straight clash between the obligation to visit the mother and straightforward self-interest. On our definition of the moral 'ought', the mother *must* be visited. But would not the vast majority of people think this would be crazy? Would not most people expect the person to collect the money? Would it not also be a ludicrous moralism to suggest that this expectation simply testifies to the slack hold that moral considerations have on us?

The trouble is that we have tried to extrapolate from certain examples in such a way as to falsify our likely reactions to very different examples such as the one we have just discussed. For example, the Good Samaritan had compassion on the man who had fallen among the thieves, while others passed by on the other side. If challenged he might well have replied, 'I simply *can't* leave him there'. In examples such as these, the overriding nature of one's moral obligations is being emphasized. The expression of necessity is itself the expression of the seriousness which the obligation has for the speaker. It is by attaching this kind of seriousness to examples which simply cannot bear it, such as the one concerning visits to the mother, that a parody of moral necessity comes about. Of course, someone may say to me that a saint might not take the money. Indeed he might not. But, then, what would it mean to make the saint's behaviour the basis for morally necessary behaviour? It is not that I want to marginalize saints and heroes as people about whom the majority need not bother their heads. Not at all. What I *am* saying is that the presence of saints and heroes cannot be used as the basis for a general view which everyone, in some obscure sense of 'must', must hold if moral necessities are to be appreciated.

In this chapter, there have been certain similarities with issues facing us in preceding chapters. In them, we start with an emaciated conception of the self and are then confronted with a sceptical challenge to show how, from this beginning, we can arrive at any firm convictions about the existence of an external world, or the existence of other human beings. In this chapter, the emaciated self with which we began was one for whom only self-interest counted. The sceptical challenge was this: How can one justify the very *possibility* of morality from such a selfish starting point? As we have seen, some philosophers accept the challenge on its own terms and argue that morality is a form of enlightened self-interest. Others, reacting against such a view, stress the contrast between moral duty and inclination, denying that moral matters can have anything to do with our desires. As we have seen, the result of this craving for a general account, for a definition of what morality is, is a distortion of the variety which confronts us when we reflect on moral possibilities.

8

Disagreements and Dilemmas

As we pointed out in the last chapter, we cannot proceed very far in a discussion of relations between human beings without a discussion of moral considerations. The two views of morality that we discussed, however — views which have been influential in moral philosophy — distorted or ignored the variety of moral possibilities seen in human life. We accused the two views of flying in the face of our common understanding. This appeal to a common understanding, as we have seen, may itself be misleading if interpreted in certain ways. It may itself be used to obscure varieties in human life in the name of a spurious unity. In particular, it may be used to cover up and misrepresent the fact of disagreements and dilemmas in morality, something about which very little was said in the last chapter. This is to be our topic in the present one.

Moral disagreement may be presented in such a way as to make our moral allegiances seem utterly irrational. For example, what are we to make of the undeniable truth that, faced with the same facts, people will still reach different moral conclusions? Some philosophers have argued that this shows that moral considerations have nothing to do with the facts. They are matters of decision. But then we have to ask why people come to the particular decisions that they embrace. This, we are told, is explicable in terms of the psychological disposition of the person concerned. On such a view, what becomes of moral discussion or reflection?

These are reduced to an effort to bring about a psychological change in the person that one is talking with. Some philosophers have gone as far as to say that *anything* which brings about the desired psychological change is permissable in the discussion. But is not this view the destruction of discussion? Moral reflection is reduced to propaganda. There is all the difference in the world between advancing reasons in a discussion and simply indulging in persuasive techniques in an effort to change people in the ways one wants.[1]

The objections to this point of view are not only moral but logical. It does not make sense to say that *anything* could count as a reason for or against a course of action. As we have seen, if I say that I am afraid to undertake a certain course of action, not *anything* can count as an object of fear. What I fear must constitute a danger of some kind. Then, again, not *anything* can count as danger. So the suggestion that *anything* in a discussion could be given as a reason for action is logically incoherent. We simply would not be able to make anything of what is said. If I say that a person cannot be trusted because his hair is only half-an-inch long, without some complex explanation, we would not know what to make of the assertion. The normal response would be, 'What does the length of his hair have to do with it?' Whether or not an adequate reply could be given in a particular case, the very request for further explication is itself an indication that there are limits to what can be advanced as reasons for actions.

Taking to heart the criticism concerning the reduction of discussion to propaganda, some philosophers tried once more to show how morality is independent of descriptive states of affairs. Morality, it is said, is based on principles.[2] These principles are based on our decisions to adopt them. But if the matter were left there, we would have been given no reason why we should adopt one principle rather than another. The principles must be shown to be rational. This can be shown, it is said, in terms of their universalisability. They are not principles which can vary from one individual to another. They are principles which, given that the circumstances are the same, every individual will assent to. If the awkward question is asked concerning why human beings assent to these principles, the answer is again given in terms of the psychological dispositions of human beings. The psychological dispositions of the individual, in the previous view, are replaced by the psychological dispositions said to belong to human beings as such. Of course, this is not to claim universal assent to these principles. There are some who adhere to principles which the vast majority of human beings would not assent to. We call this minority fanatics. There is no logical objection to fanaticism, it is said, but fanatics are cut off from most human beings – hence their name.

On the previous view we considered, discussion was reduced to propaganda. What does discussion look like on this view? It is said that we apply our normative principles to specific situations. We have to be sure that the specific situation does fall under the principle. When this is determined, we can reach a moral conclusion about that situation. The model for moral judgement looks like this:

Lying is wrong (Moral principle)
This is lying (Statement of fact)
This is wrong (Moral conclusion)

What happens if we ask for a justification of the moral principle itself? This can be provided in terms of a more fundamental moral principle, in terms of which the present principle is justified. The same question may be asked of *that* moral principle. A chain of justifications develops, in the course of which no moral principle can be cited twice. In the end we reach the most fundamental principle of all which is a matter, then, for our decision. The pattern of one more fundamental justification than the one given above would be this:

Whatever is contrary to the common good is wrong (Moral principle)
Lying is contrary to the common good (Statement of fact)
Lying is wrong (Moral conclusion)

Against such a view, it has been said that if, in the end, everything depends on a decision of principle, the whole string of justifications, however long, is 'arbitrary'. Defenders of the view have replied that this is an odd sense of arbitrary. The fundamental decision of principle referred to is a decision to adopt a whole way of life. No further reason can be given for doing so, because every reason that *could* be offered *has* been offered in the chain of justifications. What has been elucidated, in fact, is a whole way of life. In the end it must be up to an individual to decide whether or not he adopts that way of life.

But there are logical objections to this view of moral principles which are akin to the logical objections to the earlier view. The attempt to define moral principles in purely formal terms is doomed to failure. The trouble is that we can think of thousands of examples of principles which, although fulfilling these formal requirements, have nothing to do with morality.[3] Think of 'Never wear brightly coloured clothes' or 'Always were a hat on Wednesdays'. There is no difficulty in universalizing these principles. We may adopt them and be prepared to ask everyone else to do the same. But they have nothing whatever to do with morality. It is important to note what has to happen in order that such principles may be seen to have some moral point. Take 'Never wear brightly coloured clothes'. It may be that the context in which this is said concerns the values of a Puritan ethic. Wearing brightly coloured clothes is seen as ostentatious. Once the notion of ostentation is introduced, we can see some moral point in saying, 'Never wear brightly coloured clothes'. So whatever principle is advanced, unless it has a connection with *some* concepts in a range of moral concepts – truth, kindness, loyalty, generosity, and so on – the principle would have no moral point. I think this argument is sound. It would allow for the variety in moral possibilities, not only in the different priorities given to the same moral concepts, but in the fact that moral concepts present in some possibilities may be absent from others.

Unfortunately, this philosophical criticism of the view that we decide what are moral principles does not remain at this stage, but seeks to become far more ambitious. In combatting a view which gives 'decision' a false place in moral matters, it puts forward a view which threatens to give it no place at all. It has been claimed that what is right or wrong is no more a matter for decision than whether someone has a broken leg. How do philosophers reach this surprising conclusion?

We have seen how it has been argued that not anything can count as a moral possibility. To be a possibility at all, it must be related to some member at least of a wide range of moral concepts. The difficulty emerges when an attempt is made to change these concepts into a definite set of criteria for determining what is right and wrong, good and evil. Anxious to avoid making morality a matter of decision, the aim is to show that there are criteria for what can be called a good or bad action. Of course, an attempt has been made to do this in one of the most famous of moral theories, utilitarianism.[4] It was said that good actions are those which lead to the greatest happiness of the greatest number. Here we seem to be offered an external criterion to test the validity of various moral possibilities. There are various difficulties about this view, only one of which is mentioned here. It constitutes an attempt to produce a non-moral measure for moral considerations. We have already seen the difficulties that this involved for the attempt to reduce morality to enlightened self-interest. They resurface here in an attempt to define a moral action as that which leads to the greatest happiness of the greatest number. It is clear that the most despicable action may lead to this result, since what makes the greatest number happy, on this view, is not itself a moral matter. As if in part realization of this difficulty, it has been suggested that moral ends are part of what we mean by happiness. The difficulty is that a thousand rogues will disagree.

, Another attempt is made to determine criteria for the moral life, which claims to circumvent this difficulty. If the point of moral action is neither self-interest, nor the greatest happiness of the greatest number, what *is* the point of it? Surely this question must have an answer. There is no merit in saying that the point of doing something is that it is moral, without showing what the point of saying *that* is. It seems, too, that it is no longer enough to say that an action should be carried out because it would be truthful, kind, generous or loyal to do so, because someone may ask why any of these reasons have a point. The search seems to be for a justification of a moral action which satisfies and brings to an end the question 'What is the point of that?' Such a justification is found, it is argued, in an appeal to human good and harm. The actions which ought to be pursued are those which lead to human good, and the actions which ought not to be undertaken are those which lend to human harm. The question 'What is the point of achieving human good and avoiding human harm?' is pointless. We seem to have found a resting-place where no further justification is necessary. But have we?

We have seen how some philosophers have wanted to say that what is good or evil cannot be a product of our decision. Such a claim seems to rob the distinction of its importance. The counter-claim that we are considering says that we cannot decide what is good and evil since, if that distinction is rooted in a conception of human good and harm, *not anything* can count as human good and harm. Of course, because of circumstances, it may be difficult to discern what constitutes human good and harm. Partiality, prejudice and the sheer complexity of situations may get in the way. If these matters are not resolved, the disagreements that they give rise to may not be resolved either. But, in reality, there can be no abiding moral disagreements on this view. If one man says that an action leads to human good and another denies it, how can they both be right? The denial of the reality of moral disagreement may strike us as a surprising conclusion. We must look in more detail at the route by which it is arrived at.[5]

The use of the word 'good', it is said, cannot be a matter of choice. We cannot simply decide to call anything good. This can be illustrated if we take as our examples certain functional words, such as 'knife'. The interesting thing about them is that if we prefix them with 'good', their function yields criteria for what is called 'good' or 'bad' in this case: a good knife cuts well, a good dessert knife spreads well – and so on. Interestingly enough, the same results obtain in some cases in which the term involved is not purely functional. 'Farmer' has been offered as an example. Criteria of 'good' and 'bad' are found, once we ask what the point of farming is. Not anything can be called 'good farming'. The hope behind the argument is obvious. The hope is to move from 'good knife' to 'good farmer' and, finally, to 'good man'. But the hope is fatally flawed.

The problem is that when we turn to moral matters, conceptions of human good and harm already have moral import. I say 'conceptions' in the plural simply because this is the case. This being so the moral imports in the different cases will also be different. This can be illustrated even by one of the examples thought to be unproblematic. The point of farming seems obvious if we concentrate on the yield of good crops. But what if we take dairy farming as our example? Let us imagine that whether cows are grazing in the fields or kept in confined conditions does not affect the milk yield. Farmers will disagree over whether keeping cows in the latter way constitutes good farming. This disagreement cannot be resolved by an appeal to the point of farming – if by that is meant the milk yield – since that is the same in each case.

Let us consider some other examples. Injury, it may be said, is a clear example of human harm. If an action leads to an injury then that is, at least, *a* consideration against it. There is no point in asking whether injury is a bad thing. A person's need of hands, arms, eyes, and so on, is not a contingent good. Human beings need these if they are to need anything at all. This point is well taken. It is an important one in countering the suggestion that what can be called good is a matter of choice. But it does not take us to the elimination of moral disagreement which seems to be hoped for. The point about injuries can be made in a general way only because certain circumstances are being taken for granted in making it. These circumstances are extensive, so that when we hear that someone has been injured we understand that something bad has happened to that person. But such circumstances cannot always be taken for granted. There are subcultures in which violence predominates, in which injuries are displayed as scars of battle. In other warrior cultures, the practices in which injuries are displayed with pride and honour may not be subcultural at all. When a warrior is captured, the inflicting of injury on him may be seen by the warrior and the person inflicting the injury as a sign of respect. In being captured the warrior is in danger of losing his honour. The bearing of pain without flinching in a ritual in which he is given the opportunity of doing so, is the means by which his honour is recognized by his captors and retained by him. The account of a practice very different from our own does not entail our moral agreement with it. Some may wish that such warrior virtues were more prevalent in our own society. Others may be horrified at such practices, and hope fervently that missionaries or others who visit such parts of the world will endeavour to bring them to an end. Others, again, may not feel the need to pass moral judgement on the practice, emphasizing the importance of not describing it as torture. These people will disagree with each other. I do not see how any appeal to the fact that injury is said to be a bad thing in wide-ranging circumstances will do anything to settle the dispute. Neither will an appeal to human good and harm be of any use. Should such an appeal be made in the course of the dispute, the appeal would itself be to *a certain moral conception* of human good and harm, one in dispute with rival moral conceptions which think of human good and harm in different ways.

I have said that the appeal to injury as a bad thing would be understood in wide-ranging circumstances. That is certainly true, but with respect to the resolution of moral disagreements even this fact can be overestimated. The various subcultures that I alluded to aside, it would be odd to speak of people seeking out injury. I suppose various attitudes on a battlefield would have to be borne in mind as exceptions too. But given that unsought for injuries and ailments have occurred, there is still the question of how they are taken up in the rest of a person's life. Here we will meet with a wide variety of reactions, in some of which it may be denied that the injury which has happened is a bad thing. We hear of saints and others who suffer from various ailments, or thorns in the flesh, and who do not seem to emphasize getting rid of them. They say that these ailments are blessings which serve to remind them that they are not sufficient unto themselves. There are also such examples where the physical affliction is extreme. One philosopher who went blind in old age denied that what had happened to him was a bad thing when others sympathized with him. He said that he had suffered from a lack of concentration, not giving himself sufficiently to the task at hand in his work.

Now, in his blindness, he found he was able to do so. Sometimes, when disagreements occur about such matters, one protagonist finds it hard to believe that the other has fully appreciated the injury involved. I recall a televised debate between someone who called himself a rational secularist and a Roman Catholic housewife with regard to abortion. She had a large number of children already and had been told by the doctor that it would be dangerous if she had any more. She certainly did not intend to have any more children and would endeavour to avoid this happening by whatever means her faith allowed. But she went on to say that if she did find she was pregnant, there was no question of saving her life if it was a choice between her and her baby. The rational secularist was astounded. He kept emphasizing her responsibilities to the children that she already had, the dangers not only to her health, but to her life, and the moral responsibility to control the world's population. Apart from the last point, he was telling her things that she already knew about and took seriously. But she also spoke of other things: the absolute value of a life, the privilege of being a mother and the mystery of creation. It seemed to me that while she understood what the secularist meant by harm, he had little idea of what she was talking about. It is hard to see how this disagreement can be resolved by appealing to human good and harm, and to what all men want. The secularist appeals to certain considerations, but the Roman Catholic housewife wants different things. But she does not believe because she wants; she wants because she believes.

When we appreciate that different conceptions of human good and harm may already have moral import, this has implications for the dispute between those who say that what we regard as principles depends on our decisions, and those who say that such principles must be justified in terms of what all human beings want; namely, human good and harm. These implications can be appreciated in terms of the distinction between facts and values. According to the first view, there is *always* a gap between facts and values. This is insisted on in order to emphasize that, given the same facts, different moral conclusions may be drawn from them. According to the second view, there is *never* a gap between facts and values. This is insisted on in order to emphasize that, given certain facts, certain moral conclusions *must* follow. But both views feed off the deficiencies of the other.

Against the first view, it can be shown not only that moral conclusions can follow from the facts, but that our moral perspectives often determine what we take the facts to be. Take the example of seeing a frail person being set on by three thugs, who run away at one's approach. It is odd even to speak of *reaching a conclusion* from the facts if what you do is to react immediately to help the person in distress. But it can be said that the moral reaction is immediate once you see what happened. Where is the gap that must exist between facts and values? There is no gap. Moreover, moral considerations enter into one's description of what one sees. The person is seen as *frail*, as being *beaten up*, by *thugs*. The victim is said to be in *distress*. Against the second view, it can be shown that the same facts, a person being beaten up by thugs, do not *guarantee* the moral reaction that we have described. A person may morally despise the victim. This is because, once again, a moral perspective determines how the situation is seen. A frail weakling, incapable of defending himself like a man, is beaten up by thugs. Such a person deserves no pity. Suffering does not happen to a man. Or again, think of the dispute between the rational secularist and the Roman Catholic mother. Although they can agree on certain facts, their moral reactions to them are very different.

The conclusion we have come to is this. Moral reactions or moral conclusions certainly follow from facts. But what we have to remember is that such reactions and conclusions occur within certain moral perspectives. When the moral perspectives are different, different reactions will occur and different conclusions will be drawn. This conclusion does justice to the variety of moral possibilities which the other two views distort or ignore.

But where does this leave the issue of moral disagreement? It leaves it at the stage at which we can appreciate, philosophically, what such disagreement involves. But perhaps this conclusion is disappointing. Some were looking not for an appreciation of moral disagreement, but for a resolution of it. Why should it be thought that philosophy should lead to that result? A failure to do so, it may be argued, leads to a number of sceptical conclusions which seem to rob morality of its importance. First, if we cannot say that one moral point of view is better than another, it follows that they are all equal. In that case, why should one choose one rather than another? Second, if philosophy cannot provide or point to a common measure of some kind by which we can assess which moral perspective is right, how do we know to which we should give our allegiance? Perhaps the perspective I think is right is wrong, and the one I think is wrong is right. Without a common measure, how will I ever know?

These sceptical conclusions are confused. The first conclusion actually contradicts the argument that it is supposed to follow from. On the one hand, we are told that there is no common measure by which moral perspectives can be measured. On the other hand, we are told that they are all 'equal', which – of course – would be one result from such measurement. Furthermore, if we recognize that there are different moral perspectives, we cannot do so without recognizing that some of them are *related critically* to others. In that case, what would it mean to call them all equal? The remark would be quite meaningless.

What of the second sceptical conclusion, which says that if no common measure exists by which different moral perspectives may be assessed, I can never know which is right and which is wrong? From whose mouth is this confession supposed to come? Who is it who asks, 'Is what I am doing right?' We can imagine the question being asked in a real context of moral doubt or perplexity. But, apparently, when the philosopher asks the question it is not occasioned by such doubt or perplexity. It may be said that the philosopher's question arises from a philosophical confusion, the main feature of which is a failure to recognize that the question 'Is what I am doing right?' *is itself a moral question.* Think of situations in which the question is asked seriously and what an answer to it might be. I may have become doubtful about certain moral views that I used to hold strongly. What has made me doubtful? Other ways of looking at things, other moral considerations. In other words, if I call my old views mistaken, what I mean by 'mistake' will itself be elucidated in moral terms. Someone may suggest that this makes allegiance or change in moral matters a matter of taste, like either liking or not liking strawberry jam. But this suggestion cannot be sustained. It takes no account of the role of reflection and reasons in moral change. There is no avoidance of or substitution for this exercise of moral reflection. Once this is recognized we can see that the question 'I wonder what is right?' is idle when asked in abstraction. May it not come about that after I come to a different moral view, different considerations make me change yet again? Maybe. Much will depend on the style in which I put one consideration alongside another; the integrity exhibited in the way I consider objections. These will affect whether or not I am taken seriously. But there is no by-passing this context of reflective moral discussion. If I wonder whether a certain moral view of mine can be sustained, that is because my doubt must have been morally occasioned. If that is not the case, what is the doubt about? If we try to avoid circumstances such as these in discussing what perplexity or doubt concerning good and evil – right and wrong – amount to, we are ignoring the contexts of personal moral responsibility at the same time. Moral disagreements may be of concern to us in a number of ways, but these concerns are not addressed if philosophers ignore the contexts in which being sure of a moral conviction, coming to doubt it or changing it have their sense. Philosophy cannot predict what considerations will come up in a moral discussion or how an individual will take them up into his own life. Think of the differences between people who regard saints and heroes as marginal, in the sense that it makes little sense to make their example a matter of obligation for people who cannot be described as either, and others who think of them very differently. Instead of regarding saints and heroes as morally marginal, they see them as central in their moral reflections. Think of the considerations which may enter a discussion between them. There is nothing worse, it may be said, than trying to do something for which one has no vocation. It is as important to recognize what we can never be as it is to recognize what we can do something about. But it may also be said in such a discussion that the actions of saints and heroes should not be regarded as supererogatory actions, deeds which have little significance for our day-to-day obligations. Rather than beginning with the ordinary, seeing it as the limit of the possible, why not begin with the extraordinary, that which stops us in our tracks, so that the ordinary, seen in its light, may not be misdescribed? There is no *one* outcome to this discussion, no direction dictated by philosophy. In being prepared to recognize that, philosophy at least creates a space in which serious moral discussion can be itself.

Any philosophical theory that denies the possibility of unresolved moral disagreement flies in the face of common moral experience. Such disagreement is not always due to factual ignorance, lack of imagination, prejudice, stubbornness, self-deception, and so on, although this may be the case in specific instances. The differences between people are sometimes *real* moral differences, not surface phenomena which cover a deeper agreement obscured by circumstances. People care for different things, give different moral weight to various possibilities or count as moral possibilities for them alternatives which others rule out.[6]

The reluctance to recognize that there can be moral disagreements which remain unresolved for the reasons I have mentioned is matched by a similar reluctance to recognise the possibility of moral dilemmas which do not have anything that one can call 'the right answer'; dilemmas in which, whatever one does, one is going to hurt someone.

Why should there be a reluctance on the part of philosophers to recognize this possibility? It is felt that if it is allowed, the rationality and seriousness of moral considerations are threatened. I want to show that these worries, although they are real worries, need not get a grip on us.

Moral disagreement is not a surprising phenomenon given what I have said about the variety of moral possibilities. But moral dilemmas are surely not a surprising phenomenon either. Think of the diverse movements and institutions which may contribute to shaping one's moral views. Think of the influence of values which may be called family values and the ways in which these are extended to apply in wider spheres: 'No one should treat his brother or sister like that'; 'No one should treat another member of the tribe like that'; 'No one should treat a human being like that.' Think of ideas bound up with physical labour which also come to have wider moral applications: the idea of an honest day's work and of getting a job well done. Again we have experiences affected by warfare either as participants or victims – we're all in this together and everyone must play his part. The influence of aesthetic ideals on moral character is apparent: the style of an act and someone's having a beautiful nature. This is not meant as any kind of systematic survey, obviously, but simply as some simple suggestions of the diversity of moral influences in people's lives. If we add to these and the many others we would have to mention – what distinctive contributions individuals make to our moral understanding, the particular style of a magnanimous deed from which we can learn, or the imaginative insight of a moral comment made by a wise person – why should it be at all surprising that through the play of circumstances these different values create conflicts and clashes in one's life of the kind that we call moral dilemmas?

It may be said that philosophers have not wanted to deny that these conflicts occur. What they are unhappy about is the idea that there is no answer to them. This appears, to them, to be a counsel of despair. The first thing to be said in response is that I am not arguing that no dilemma *can* be resolved. What I am saying is that room must be left in our account of dilemmas for those which are not. One may have the kind of morality in which matters have a clear priority, so that when clashes of allegiance occur there is no problem about which one has to fulfil. Fine, but in that case the person has no dilemma.

Let us suppose, however, that someone does not have a morality which has a priority for all alternatives. (We may wonder how plausible such a morality is, but let that pass.) In that case a person may well be faced with a clash of obligations. It is the characterization of this clash which has provoked philosophical disagreement.

It has seemed to some that this clash of obligations must not be stated in a form which is irrational. For example, how can *both* obligations be my duties? If duty is what ought to be done, then how can I have two duties? My duty is what I shall arrive at if I resolve the dilemma. To express these differences, philosophers have said that what clashes is not actual duties, but prima-facie duties. These latter duties indicate what tend to be your duties, not what is actually your duty. Your absolute duty is what you actually ought to do.

Philosophers who argue against this point of view say that it seems to destroy the reality of moral dilemmas. Surely, we are not torn between things which tend to be our duty, but between actual duties. Why is it thought necessary to call conflicting duties prima-facie duties? Is it not because of the mistaken assumption that a duty *must* be performed? That the assumption is mistaken can be shown by the confusions it leads to. If a duty must be performed, a right must be satisfied. In terms of dilemmas we can say that prima-facie rights clash, but the right action is the resolution of the dilemma. But why, if rights *must* be satisfied, do we speak of standing on our rights? It would be quite superfluous to do so. That it is not shows the recognition of the familiar fact that rights *compete* for satisfaction. Arguments and counter-arguments are heard and weighed. Consider another consequence. If rights are always to be satisfied, waiving one's rights would be an immoral act. But we often commend people for waiving their rights. People tell others to forget what they owe them, while undoubtedly having a right to be repaid. If this were not so, what are they telling them to forget? Again, if a right must be satisfied, a clash of rights would be a logical incoherence instead of a problem waiting to be resolved.

These obviously unacceptable conclusions are avoidable once we see that rights and duties must not necessarily be satisfied. Does this mean that there is no necessity attached to them? Not at all, but what they ask of us is *necessary consideration, not necessary satisfaction.* Thus in a moral dilemma we must consider all the moral considerations involved, but obviously we cannot satisfy them all. Which ones we do satisfy is the result of wise moral deliberation. It may be said that moral wisdom is knowing what priorities to arrive at when moral considerations clash.

This view is certainly an advance on the one it criticises. It shows the inadequacy in the conception of prima-facie duties or prima-facie rights. It is also an advance on the view that in resolving moral dilemmas what we do is to find exceptions to moral principles. It shows that in moral dilemmas we have *real* clashes between obligations, rights and duties. It is odd to think the resolution of such clashes can be expressed in terms of a moral principle followed by a long list of exceptions. The resolution is arrived at by moral reflection.

Nevertheless, the revised view is also problematic in some respects. It is optimistic in that it always seem to envisage the resolution of moral dilemmas, the arrival at the right answer. Given this view, no account can be given of the possibility of remorse, even after the resolution of a dilemma. Remorse involves saying that were circumstances to be repeated, one would not repeat the action for which one now feels remorse. There cannot be remorse without repudiation. But in the resolution of some dilemmas, this condition cannot be satisfied. Someone may do what he or she has to do, but still feel remorse for the unfulfilled obligation. But how is this possible? How can it be said, on the one hand, that this is what one must do, and yet, on the other hand, that one feels remorse for what has been left undone – or, indeed, for what had been done? To many philosophers, this does not make sense. I suggest, however, that in saying this they are ignoring a real moral possibility in some people's lives. Let us explore further what this possibility amounts to.[8]

The first thing that has to be said is that one is talking about one kind of result of a moral dilemma. Perhaps it is misleading to call it the resolution of a moral dilemma, since that gives the impression that what has been arrived at is *the* right thing to do. Someone may agonize over the question of whether he ought to leave his wife. He is aware of his obligations, but life in the marriage may be leading to a mutual destruction. He decides to leave. Years later he is able to say that he did the right thing, and not mean by this simply the right thing for himself. The way in which things work out shows that it was the right answer for the marriage too.

But it is not always like that. A man may find that there is a clash between his work and his marriage. Someone may remonstrate with him, saying that since he has taken the woman out of her family and she has made his life her own, surely he has to stick with her now. Someone else, after all, can carry on his work of cancer research. He can give it up and do something else. But matters are not so simple as that. He would give up his work but he knows the effect on himself; he knows that would drag him down and that he would drag his wife down with him. Here we have all the makings of a tragic moral conflict. Some philosophers have objected to such examples by saying that the 'no solution' has been written in to the account given of them. But it is not a case of 'writing in', but of recognizing a possible case. Things may not be as described, but, surely, they can be as described. This is what some philosophers will not admit.[9] Some argue that we can never rule out the possibility of a third alternative turning up. True, but we can never rule out the possibility of a third alternative not turning up either. What is more, we are sometimes in the position, in a given case, of knowing that such an alternative has not and cannot turn up. In the example we have considered, the man may decide to leave. He is not saying that he has *the* answer, but he does what he has to do. Again, after some time, he may be able to say that he did the right thing. But he may not. He may remain in the situation of feeling deep remorse for what he has done to his wife. It is foolish to argue, as some philosophers have done, that he can feel regret, but not remorse. His remorse is itself an expression of his recognition of what he has done. Failure by philosophers to recognize this possibility is perhaps due to a tendency on their part towards tidiness and systems. Unsurprisingly, this would lead to a failure to recognize that in life doing what we must do morally may still not free us from blame or involvement with evil. Philosophy may lead us to think we can get away without dirtying our hands, but life does not.

One obstacle to the recognition of tragic moral dilemmas is the attempt to see their resolution in terms of finding out when a rule has to be followed. Suppose that my friendship with someone has been characterized by absolute straightforwardness and truthfulness. That someone asks me to promise that if I think she is dying, I will tell her. She says that it is good, if possible, for a person to have a little time to reflect before death. I promise. But, when the time comes, I am also convinced that my friend is not up to being told – that what telling her would amount to would not be a time for reflection, but a time of terror. On one philosophical view, what I am doing is deciding that the principle of truth-telling, in this instance, does not apply. In that case, of course, how can I feel remorse or uncertainty about the broken promise? I cannot. Truth-telling, it may be said, rightly took the second place in this instance to a desire to avoid unbearable suffering.

This reasoning rests on the assumption that I do regard the situation as an exception to a rule. Of course, I may, but in this case I do not. My obligation to maintain the truthful character of my relationship with my friend retains its force. It is just that in these circumstances, I cannot fulfil it. After her death, I may wonder for the rest of my life whether I did the right thing. Did I play at being God? People react in very surprising ways when they know they are going to die. Even some who have been hypochondriacs all their lives have been known to receive and bear the knowledge with dignity and bravery. So how could I have been so sure? And so on. Yet, at the time, even if 'sure' may be too strong a word, I did make my judgement and did not think I should risk a terrified end for my friend. In the event, her end was peaceful. And yet . . .

Consider, again, the case of a religious pacifist who kills a murderer in order to save a child. He may not regard what he has done as giving priority to one principle over another, since in this instance what he did was an exception to his pacifist principles. Not at all. He thinks he has committed a great wrong. He has taken a human life. He may even say he has murdered someone, no matter what others say. Of course, he also saved a child and did not commit the other wrong in which he would have been involved; namely, of doing nothing while a child was murdered. Yet, he may feel remorse for what he has done, and think that some form of penance is required. I do not see any merit in philosophers trying to avoid cases such as these. In short, philosophy must leave room in its reflections for moral tragedies.

We saw earlier how some philosophers are reluctant to recognize moral differences. This same reluctance recurs in their discussions of moral dilemmas. Even if these dilemmas are recognized, many philosophers insist that if the rationality of morality is to be preserved, an answer to a moral dilemma *must* be an answer which *any* person would give to it.[10]

What accounts for this philosophical insistence? We can answer this question in terms of the importance of moral consistency. What I mean is this. Let us suppose that I criticize you for doing something wrong, but seek to excuse myself for doing the same thing. I would be rightly accused of hypocrisy. Furthermore, if on one day I criticized some action, but on the next day I praised it, I would be accused of inconsistency. I would be challenged to show some relevant difference between the two situations to account for my change in judgement. If none could be found, I myself would be open to criticism for the change. Indeed, if my changes of judgement were often and radical enough, no one would be able to even call what I am doing 'judging' at all. They would rightly say, 'You can't tell what he is up to from one minute to the next'. So consistency in my *own* judgements *is* extremely important if those judgements are to have any semblance of moral seriousness or, indeed, of rationality.

The philosophical view that we are considering, however, is far more ambitious than this. It does not say simply that there must be consistency between my *own* moral judgements, but that there must be consistency between my judgements and the judgements of *everyone else* made in *the same* circumstances. Just as you would not know what to make of me if my judgements varied from one moment to the next, so, it is argued, you wouldn't know what to make of moral judgements if some people resolved moral dilemmas in one way, while others resolved *the same* dilemmas in quite different ways. If this happens, the argument concludes, morality is reduced to simply doing whatever you think is right. There is no longer any question of what *is* right.

It is not difficult to predict, from what has already been said in this chapter and the previous one, that I do not think that these conclusions can survive close scrutiny. Faced with the dilemmas that we have mentioned, people have resolved them in very different ways. Similarly, my response to what another person does may vary. In certain cases, I may want to say that what a person did was right. In certain cases I may want to say that what a person did was wrong. That response, would, of course, not be acceptable to the philosophers who argue in the way we are condemning now. But that is not the response I want to discuss. I may also say of someone's response to a dilemma, 'He did what was right for him'. I want to discuss this response because it seems, at first sight, to be the very result that philosophers warned us against. In saying that someone did what was right for him, am I not saying that whatever he said was right was right, so destroying what seems to be the all-important distinction between 'what I think is right' and 'what is right'? The view that the moral conclusions I reach when faced with a dilemma must, in order to be a *moral* conclusion, accord with the conclusions anyone else would reach in the same circumstances is known as *the principle of universalizability*.

We have said enough in the present chapter to show how, faced with the same moral considerations, people will weigh them differently. The same is true in the resolution of a moral dilemma. If the way in which a person resolves a dilemma is such that it affects my moral sensibilities sufficiently, then I will say that it is wrong. But, sometimes, I may not want to judge the action right or wrong, even when I could not bring myself to do what the person has done. My reaction is expressed by saying, 'He did what was right for him'. Our question is how I can say this without the trivialization of morality, of saying 'Whatever he says is right for him is right for him.'

This trivialization can be avoided if we pay attention to the fact that there are limits to the circumstances in which we can say 'It was right for him'. For example, we could only say it of a person who is morally serious about the issues confronting him. There could be a philosophical lack of seriousness too. What if someone argued as follows: If the obligations with which a person is faced are equally important, it follows that whatever he does he is going to do what he ought to do, so it does not matter what he does. This *would* be a trivialization of the whole situation. On this view, it would be a complete mystery as to why the person has a dilemma at all! But also, if, for example, the pacifist was simply a conformist member of the sect and allowed the child to be killed simply because the rules are what they are, then we would not say that there had been any moral consideration of the matter. More grotesquely, what if someone suggested resolving a dilemma by spinning a coin? We would not dream of saying that such a person did what was right for him.

The second context in which this could not be said would be one in which the person who comes to a moral conclusion is the victim of self-deception. He may look as if he cares about what he has done, but the pattern of his behaviour shows that he is deceiving himself. We have already seen how the decision that a person takes may be so morally objectionable that we cannot bring ourselves to say that he did the right thing. These checks show that if we want to say of the way a person resolves a dilemma, 'He did what was right for him', this does not amount to saying that whatever the person did would be right. Neither the agent nor the spectators of his action think in this way.

Sometimes, those who say that a moral resolution of a dilemma must be one that anyone would reach in the same circumstances, also say that the sameness of circumstances is rare. This is because they include, in the circumstances, how they strike the individual involved. But if an individual's moral reaction is included as part of what is to count as the same circumstances, the principle of universalizability is robbed of any credibility.

During the course of the chapter, we have resisted various philosophical attempts to tidy up – and so to obscure – the moral variety confronting us when we reflect on morality. This becomes extremely important, as we have seen, if we are to do justice to the complexities involved in moral disagreements and moral dilemmas.

9

Political Obligation

In the course of our discussions we have confronted the question of how we move from a private, isolated self to any confidence in acquaintance with an external world, other human beings and moral realities. In all three contexts we reject the presuppositions from which, it was said, we have to begin.

The same issues arise when we consider political obligation. We have to face the same sceptical challenge. According to this challenge it is not *possible* to speak intelligibly of an external world, human beings or moral considerations. In this chapter we have to face the challenge of whether we can speak intelligibly of political obligation.

How does this become a matter of doubt? There is no one answer to this question. I am going to explore one well-known route by which such doubt can be created. If we assume that the centre of sense-experience is the mind of the individual, a mind sufficient unto itself to understand what it received, it is natural to ask why it is that individuals are found living in societies. Individuals are natural, but societies, it seems, are not. Society seems to be a conventional arrangement in which individuals have chosen to live. But this simply postpones the question: Why should they have chosen to do so?

If society is an unnatural convention, and if it makes sense to ask why people live in this way, it is very difficult to avoid the suggestion that before people lived in societies, they lived in some other state. This pre-social existence has been called *the state of nature*. Our question then becomes: Why did people move from a state of nature to a social state?

In a state of nature, it is said, the individual is moved by appetites and aversions. Persons will want to satisfy their appetites to the full. But since the strength of each individual is roughly the same, people in a state of nature are in a constant state of strife or potential strife. The state of nature is therefore a state of contradiction. Every individual wants to fulfil appetites and enjoy them in peace, only to find the situation an unavoidable state of antagonism, with everyone pitted against everyone else and death an ever-present danger. In fact, it has been said that life will be nasty, brutish and short.

What did people do to deliver themselves from this unfortunate situation? They disciplined their unrestrained appetites. They no longer said they had a right to everything. They all agreed to subject themselves to a sovereign, a political power who would ensure that contracts between individuals were kept. Given what we have said about the unrestrained appetites of individuals, these contracts would never be kept without the external authority of the sword. Without the sword the covenants that people make with each other would be empty words, for what would ensure the efficiency of the covenants? The only reason for not obeying the sovereign is when it becomes evident that the sovereign can no longer keep the peace necessary for covenants to be honoured.[1]

What are we to make of this analysis? What kind of analysis is it – historical? anthropological? It does not have any credibility as either, despite the fact that some philosophers thought that states of nature probably described the lives led by distant tribes. The reference to states of nature is understood by some, not as a reference to a past pre-social state, but as a warning about the state that society can fall into if political order is not observed. In this respect, attention is drawn to the fact that most political philosophers, in advancing their theories, have been influenced by the political events of their day.

No doubt there is something to be said for all these suggestions, but they by-pass the fundamental philosophical issues. The reference to the state of nature is understood best from a philosophical perspective, as an analysis of political obligation. If people are born free, why are they in chains? The analysis that we have considered should be seen as an answer to that question. If you want to understand political obligation, the way to do so is to begin with the psychology of the individual. It is by beginning with the appetites and aversions of the individual that we will come to understand why we subject ourselves to political obligation.

The trouble is, however, that the offered transition from a state of nature to society is inherently problematic. We are told that no agreements can be kept unless we have a sovereign to ensure that they are kept. The very notion of agreement is said to depend on the sovereign. But, in that case, how could people be said *to have agreed* to have a sovereign? The agreement to have a sovereign seems to falsify the need for the sovereign. If the *possibility* of agreement depends on a sovereign, how could there have been agreement – prior to the existence of a sovereign – to have one? This is a major criticism of the analysis. But even if we put this objection aside, the relation with the sovereign which is said to come into existence cannot account for political obligation. According to the analysis, why should we obey the sovereign? Two possible motives suggest themselves. First, we may have prudential reasons for obeying the sovereign. That much is obvious from the reasons why one wants to escape from the state of nature. Second, we may have to obey the sovereign out of necessity. The sovereign's resources are far greater than ours. But whether we obey the sovereign out of prudence or necessity, this is not the same as a sense of political obligation. Given the limits of the story of the transition from a state of nature to a society, no account can be given of obligation.

This criticism has been made by philosophers who have seen that political obligation can never be arrived at from the self-interested starting-point in the state of nature.[2] They have not abandoned the notion of a state of nature, but deny that people are only motivated by self-interest within it. Moral considerations, it is said, are already in operation in the state of nature. So why, on this revised view, do people move from a state of nature to society? Their answer relies on the absence of any institutional or legal procedures in a state of nature. There is no way of arbitrating disputes if they occur in a state of nature. These only develop in society.

There is also a fundamental change in the notion of a contract in this revised view. In the previous view, there is no contract between the people and the sovereign. They surrender their right to everything to the sovereign. But the consequence, as we have seen, is that no account can be given of political obligation. In the revised view, matters are very different. The contract is between the people and the sovereign. If the sovereign does not meet the political obligations in the contract, the sovereign can be removed. That is why, unlike the first view, this revised view is a genuine *social contract theory*. The government of the sovereign is not the result of a surrender of rights by people, but the result of their explicit consent.[3]

The answer to the question of why we are subject to political obligations on this view is that we have consented to this subjection. But what have we consented to? When we begin to answer this question, many difficulties begin to emerge. There is the general problem of how a contract supposedly made by our ancestors is able to bind us *now*. Furthermore, how is this original consent made by people we never knew related to the specific matters concerning which our political consent is sought? The attempt to answer this question leads us to some of the most fundamental issues in political philosophy.

Let us begin by considering the results of a parliamentary vote. What does it mean to say that people have consented to this result? If they are among those members of parliament who actually voted for the measures, the answer is straightforward. But what of the members who voted against the measures? In what sense can they be said to have consented to them? The answer offered is that although they obviously have not consented explicitly to the measures passed, they have given tacit consent to them by consenting explicitly to abide by the results of a certain voting procedure. What of the wider electorate, who have not taken any part in the voting procedure? The answers given are very similar. Those of the electorate who voted for the party who voted for the measures have delegated the right to make political decisions to them. Those who voted for the party who voted against the measures again are said to have given their tacit consent by consenting to the political process. But what of people who have not taken part in the voting? They are said to have consented to the political procedures simply by walking the king's or queen's highway. If they do not want to live in the country in which they reside, they need not do so. It has been said that this is like saying to people in a boat in the middle of an ocean that if they do not like it they can always get out.

Whatever we make of these answers, how are they related to the main feature of social contract theory – *the original contract?* The issue of how an original agreement can or should bind us now remains a mystery. Even if it could be said that there had been an original consent to some political system or other, how would *that* consent justify the continuation of that system? But, it has been asked, where is this original contract? When did this original agreement take place? Where can it be found? It has been asked whether it can be found written on parchment or on the bark of trees, since there is certainly no record of it. Furthermore, if we think of various political traditions of sovereignty, explicit consent plays no part in them. For example, consider sovereignty by inheritance. Where is the explicit consent by the people in that? People will recognize that someone is the legitimate heir to the throne, but would be very puzzled if asked what role their consent played in any of it. But, at various times in history, sovereignty has not been by inheritance, but by conquest. It would, of course, be absurd to suggest that consent played any part in that. Furthermore, the reaction of people to being conquered is decidedly mixed. In some cases, the conqueror is hated and even though he may reign for a very long time, when he is at last overthrown, the rightful heir is welcomed back with rejoicing. Even so, the people do not think that the fact that there is a rightful heir depends in any way on their explicit consent. At other times in history, the conqueror has been preferred to the rightful heir, who may be hated by his people. But there is still no room for the people's explicit consent here.

It seems, then, that there are insuperable difficulties facing any social contract theory when questions of this kind are put to it. But should we leave matters there? It may be that what the social contract theory wanted to say cannot be said, but perhaps what it tried to say is connected with something that needs to be said.

In some way, the social contract theory wanted to suggest that what we do in a specific political action is somehow connected with something wider than itself, and that this connection must have something to do with consent or agreement. I think something important is being said here which is worth exploring. In order to so do, we have to distinguish between consent and *prior* consent.[4]

It is very difficult when we speak of *consent* not to think of voting, or of the various examples of tacit consent that we have discussed which are connected with voting procedures. Of course, this is one example of consent, by which I mean a political system, a way of going about things that we go along with. The central issue here is *legitimacy*. The people regard the political procedures as legitimate. But the political systems that people have responded to in this way are far more varied than systems of parliamentary democracy. We have already seen this from the examples that we have mentioned in this chapter. Take the recognition of a rightful king and a readiness to fight for him. Why have many gone along with this? Simply because he is the king. Yet, this does not mean that we can reduce legitimacy to legality. During the German occupation of France in the Second World War, the Vichy government was the legal government, and, yet, throughout the country there was no sense of it as the legitimate government. It lacked all moral authority.[5]

It is difficult to spell out what is involved in the notion of legitimacy, since it will depend on factors which will vary, perhaps dramatically, with different political traditions. For those within traditions of parliamentary democracy it may be difficult to recognize that there *are* these different factors which will account for different conceptions of legitimacy. If you believe in the divine right of kings, a vote taken by parliament will not impress you.

These different political traditions are the necessary background if we want to give an account of political discussion. Before elaborating this important fact, however, we have to modify it immediately.

We cannot assume that any notion of political legitimacy gives an important place to discussion. In this respect, the examples that remind us of sovereignty by conquest are extremely important. This is because some philosophers are tempted to think that such conduct is irrational! The contrast between high cultures and barbaric hordes obscures what needs to be recognized; namely, that marauding hordes have values and traditions of their own, although discussion is not high among them. Philosophers unable to recognize this fact have claimed that their activities could be shown to be irrational by appeal to rights which belong to the political systems with which they are familiar and want to advocate. For example, the glorification of the tribe in the way prisoners are dealt with by many tribes may appal its 'rational' critics. These philosophers claim that if they could reason with such people they could get them to see that they were acting irrationally, causing gratuitous pain, and so on. The spectacle is a rather comic one. The rational argument would soon, I fear, come to a violent end. The point is not that there is any philosophical objection to criticizing the warrior people. The criticism will be rooted in certain moral and political values. I repeat: there is no objection to that. The objection is to the confused assumption that the warriors' values are really confusions of or deviations from these moral and political values. What needs to be recognized is that the values are what the warriors say they are, and discussion may not be rated highly among them. In short, using the term 'political' in a wide sense, we have to recognize that there may be a radical clash between different political systems. Of course, those who cherish democratic values may hope that change comes about through the kind of discussion associated with those values. In fact, that may not happen. Change may come about through conquest, or because the rest of the world surrounding the ways of the warriors simply smothers them out of existence.

It may be thought that such examples are too remote. What we ought to concentrate on now is the kind of political discussion carried on between governments, which stands in some relation to political rules which govern the international community. But the example may not be as remote as we think. Think of the recent experience of the break-up of communist control in Eastern Europe. At the time, there were liberal hopes that, after the years of oppression, democracy would prevail. What happened in many of the countries was that voting often conformed to old ethnic divisions. Many were disappointed with these developments, but the clash between the real divisions and the electoral system within which they expressed themselves is extremely instructive. To some observers in the West, the electoral system is the reality and the ethnic conformity is the distortion. But is not the reverse nearer the truth, whatever we may think of it? The realities are the ethnic differences, and the electoral system is a feature of a political context which the countries were not ready for and, perhaps, did not want.

This has an important bearing on the notion of legitimacy. Consider examples of democratic practices imposed on tribal communities. Despite the fact that members of the tribe take part in an electoral system, they vote as their chief or elders tell them to vote. Given this situation, can we speak of a legitimate electoral system? Surely not. People could not be said to consent to it. What does saying this mean? It means that the ideas bound up with electoral systems play no real part in their lives, no matter what overt reactions they go through. They may go to the polling booths, collect voting slips, and put a cross opposite a name or names, but what does any of it mean to them? The ideas that enter their lives, that mean something to them, are found in the tribal systems. Unless that happens to political ideas, there is no sense of legitimacy and the political procedures remain external to the people.

I have digressed somewhat to speak of the politics of tribal systems or ethnic groupings, in order to show that if we think that political philosophy's task is to define 'legitimacy', we shall run into the same difficulties as those we discussed in the chapters on moral philosophy. Once we provide a definition of a good action, we found, inevitably, examples of actions called 'good' which cannot be captured by the definition. The result will be the same if we try to define political legitimacy. We have noted extreme differences in order to emphasize this, differences which – as we have seen – may not even recognize the importance of discussion.

Noting these differences allows us to distinguish between different contexts for saying 'It is legitimate'. In one context we are making a political judgement. We say of some political practice, or, indeed, of a government as such, that it is or is not legitimate. In saying this we are showing where we stand politically. But in other contexts, when we say 'This is legitimate' we are making a descriptive remark about what is held to be legitimate in this or that political system. No doubt, as in the moral cases, where we stand ourselves politically may limit what we are prepared to countenance as an example of political legitimacy in a political system, but there is still an important distinction between the two contexts. We have already seen the importance of not conflating them in political philosophy.

For example, it is only by noting the *different* conceptions of political legitimacy that we can bring out the confusions in thinking that legitimacy can be based on some conception of rationality which determines its nature and essence. Reminding ourselves of the differences is also important for the light it throws on the vital distinction that we noted before we began this digression – the distinction between consent and prior consent.

As we have seen, the social contract theories we considered at the outset of this chapter all depend on the notion of *prior* consent. This led, naturally, to issues concerning when this consent was given, and how such an original consent, given by our fathers in the mists of time, could have any bearing on our political obligations now. These issues, I have argued, cannot be resolved satisfactorily. So serious are the difficulties connected with them that we have to give up the notion of prior consent as irredeemably confused. But that does not mean that the notion of consent is unimportant. On the contrary, by reflecting on different political systems we see the difference between *prior consent to them and consenting in them*. The difficulty with prior consent in relation to ourselves is that we have no recollection of having given any such consent. We were born at a certain time into certain political systems. Their existence had nothing to do with us. But there is still the question of whether we can find our feet in them. This is not a consent that we give prior to the political activities, but one that shows itself *in* our involvement in these activities. The political issues matter to us, we argue for or against certain measures, and so on. Notice that the notion of consent that I am talking about is wider than the specific consent that I give to a political measure that I happen to agree with. Social contract theories tried to account for this difference in terms of the distinction between explicit and tacit consent. I am suggesting that we can bring out the distinction between the specific consent that I give to a political measure and the consent shown in what I take to be political discussion and involvement, without which my specific consent would make no sense.

It may seem that what I am saying about this wider concept of consent is conservative and allows no room for the notion of reform. This comes from my remark that what I consent to exists before I am born and my consent is simply my willing involvement in it. But, surely, in the case of the reformer, things are very different. What the reformer wants to bring about does not already exist and, to that extent, he or she is not at home in the political system in which he or she finds him- or herself. This is true, but strengthens the importance of the notion of consent I am trying to elucidate. This can be brought out if we emphasize that political reform does not occur in the abstract. Unless it took place in a wider political context it would not have any significance as a reform. If we want to change something politically, it will be in a context in which there are many things which one does not want to change. Even in situations, as with political parties, in which people differ about what they want to change, there will be matters not on the political agenda as far as change is concerned. If we ever ask someone what he or she wants to change and the reply is 'Everything' we can be assured that that person lacks political seriousness.

It may be argued that these conclusions only apply to political reforms within a political system; the kind of system within which parties of different political persuasion may exist. But what of revolutionaries? Surely, they are talking of overthrowing a political system, not of reforms within it. This is true, and history has shown us that the changes may be very great. But, as in the case of a specific reform, a revolution does not take place in a political vacuum. It often proclaims ideals, already known, which – it is said – have been neglected or distorted. More ambitiously, it may speak in terms of a latent ideal which it claims to be bringing into existence for the first time. In a political vacuum, however, revolutions could not have the seriousness that they possess.

It may still be thought that my conclusions will only account for disputes within a political system or for revolutions which still invoke conceptions of the state. But what of anarchists who speak of overthrowing the state? Do not their ambitions rob us of the wider context in which I have spoken of political consent? I do not think it does, although the change envisaged is even greater than that involved in the other revolutions that we have mentioned. And yet, even when we are speaking of the overthrow of the state, it is important to remember that anarchists recognize the political importance of what they are opposing. Furthermore, in the political arrangements that are envisaged which do not involve the institution of the state, there is not complete discontinuity with what is overthrown.

These matters are made all the more complicated by the fact that what can and cannot be changed politically is not itself a rigid distinction. What is not on the agenda for political change in one generation, may be on such an agenda in another generation. The important point is that political philosophy cannot determine such matters. The philosophical point is that in any serious political discussion or political movement, not everything can be questioned. There will always be some political considerations which, at any one time, can be taken for granted. It is in such a context that any political activity – conservative, reformist or revolutionary – has sense.[6]

It may be thought that what I have said gives too little attention to the personal in politics. This was certainly not my intention.

For example, if we think again of the deep demoralization in France under the Vichy government and of its subsequent liberation, it would be difficult to overestimate the importance of General De Gaulle in the latter context. He carried in his person, it might be said, an incomparable moral and political authority. Nothing I have said is meant to deny this. But the wider political context in which our consent shows itself is essential to that context in which De Gaulle's authority or that of any person is possible. This does not mean that his authority is reducible to this wider context. That *would* be to eliminate the importance of persons in politics. But a political genius is no more isolatable from a wider political tradition than an artistic genius is isolatable from a wider artistic tradition, even though the genius may be related sympathetically or unsympathetically to the tradition.

Throughout our discussions in this chapter, we have been concerned to meet the sceptical challenge: How is political obligation possible? We have argued that it cannot be arrived at from the starting-point of the self-interest of individuals. We have also argued that political life cannot be explained in terms of a prior consent on the part of our ancestors to engage in it. Political life does not have a contractual basis. As we have seen, that does not mean that the notion of consent is unimportant. We have concentrated on the consent which shows itself *in* the political activity in which we are engaged; in what we go along with and appeal to in our discussions. This kind of consent is related to the wide contexts we have talked of, contexts in which a spectrum of political activity, however varied, has its sense. Where people stop in offering justifications in these contexts varies − sometimes a great deal. There are co-operative and unco-operative relations between different political movements which have different political ideals. Yet, as we have seen, conflict as well as co-operation requires something fixed, without which neither would have political sense or seriousness. Some philosophers have suggested that in determining what political state is desirable, details such as those I have alluded to are irrelevant. They are the arbitrary results of historical circumstances. What we need is to ignore such factors and return to more rational deliberation. A thought-experiment will enable us to do this. We could imagine human beings behind a veil of ignorance which keeps from them all knowledge of their social status, their privileges, the social movements to which they belong, and so on. From this starting-point, behind the veil of ignorance, denuded of all such details, we could begin, through reflection, to arrive at those interests and social arrangements which would constitute the common good.[7] But if the arguments of this chapter amount to anything, such a project will have been shown to be fatally flawed. The original position behind the veil of ignorance will be seen to be as vacuous a notion as prior consent. If we are placed behind the veil of ignorance, so far from being given a position from which rational discussion may commence, we have been separated from those contexts in which the very possibility of serious political activity or discussion is found. Such activity and discussion may often involve different political movements which exhibit different political ideals and ideas. These ideas and ideals are not approximations to or hypotheses about something called the common good. They are what they are, and that is what we need to recognize if we are to appreciate political disputes. An appeal to the common good is often no more than the illegitimate elevation of *one* of these movements. It has been said that society could not go on if different movements were to pursue their distinctive interests: to which it has been rightly replied, 'That is how it *does* go on'. The aim of this chapter has been to show how, in the context of political life, that is so.[8]

10

Aesthetic Values

To turn from considerations in political philosophy to considerations in aesthetics may seem, at first, to be a turn from the most
public to the most private of concerns. Whereas politics has to do
with the affairs of a tribe, a city or a country, aesthetics, it may be
said, is a matter of individual tastes. It has to do with how people
react to the visual arts, music and literature. It is true that just as
there have been attempts in moral philosophy and political
philosophy to define the essence of moral or political obligation,
so there have been attempts to define the essence of aesthetic
appreciation. What does it mean to speak of a good painting, a
good piece of music or a good work of literature? What are we
looking for when we try to answer this question?

One way in which some philosophers have tried to answer this
question is to try to locate some property in the work of art which
makes us call it 'good'. This should remind you of our discussions
in the first three chapters. There we discussed the conception of
the self as the passive recipient of sense-experiences. We were
then invited to consider how, from this inner world of experience,
we can ever talk with any confidence of an external world. We
saw that this picture is fatally flawed. One of the difficulties
concerning it is the idea that we could have an idea of something
just by confronting it. For example, the suggestion that simply by
confronting something in certain conditions I would have the
impression 'red'. The same is supposed to occur in the case of

every individual. But, here – as we saw – a sceptical challenge appears. How can I ever know that the impression I receive is the same impression that you receive? How do I know whether what I mean by 'red' is the same experience as the one you call 'red'? We came to the conclusion that we can only see our way out of this scepticism by rejecting the presuppositions on which it is based. Without repeating the arguments here, we came to see the importance of common reactions in the determination of the meaning of 'red'. It is only in the context of such common reactions that you and I come to this meaning. We may find similar considerations – despite important differences – emerging in our discussion of aesthetic values.

Consider the example of looking at a painting. According to the view under consideration, if I have normal eyesight and look at it in normal light conditions, it will create an impression on me. Certain paintings create on me the impression I call 'beautiful' and that is why I call the painting 'good'. But – as with the case of sense-experience – on this view, how can we ever know that two people are having the *same* impression when they say that a painting is beautiful? In the case of our use of 'beautiful', the analogy with seeing red begins to limp. Although common reactions are important in the aesthetic context too, they are not the kind of reactions by which the meaning of colour words is determined. The reactions which have to do with colours are not learned or acquired. We react in a certain way and find that others agree in the case of the colour we call 'red'. But aesthetic values are acquired. To appreciate a painting, the way it is looked at must be a *trained* look. What is more, the distinctions such a training involves are far too complex to be captured in a catch-all word such as 'beautiful'.

Before developing this matter further, let us explore how a very different account of aesthetic appreciation comes about. Realizing the difficulties in the view which tries to argue that 'beauty' is a property in paintings, some have concluded that these difficulties come from the search for such properties. What we have to realize is that appreciation here is a matter of personal choice, a matter of taste. One person likes a painting while, another does not – what more is there to say? But this makes aesthetic likes and dislikes akin to likes and dislikes concerning strawberry jam. It leaves no room for the possibility of discussion and reflection. But just as we saw, when discussing moral matters, that not anything can be called good, so not anything can be the object of the various words that we may use to convey our appreciation of a painting.

The two alternative views of aesthetic appreciation that we have considered suffer from the same lack: the ignoring of the cultural context in which this appreciation has its sense. On the first view, a painting causes the observer to have an experience described as 'beautiful' or 'ugly'. There is no room here to ask why this should be so. Neither is there any room to ask what might be meant by calling one impression deeper than another. On the second view, the observer simply chooses to call the painting beautiful. Why one painting should be chosen rather than another cannot be explained, since any evaluation offered would itself simply be a product of choice.

What is missing in each case is the essential place of a cultural tradition in which our judgements have their sense. What I mean can be brought out by considering the example of a great painting. Each view we have considered feeds off the deficiency of the other. The emphasis on properties wants to preserve the obvious truth that the greatness of the painting tells us something, not about ourselves, but about the painting. We can speak of learning something from a great painting. It would be extremely ego-centric to say that what I learn is always something about myself. The emphasis on choice and taste, on the other hand, wants to preserve the emphasis on judgement, on the fact that the appreci-ation of a great painting is not the passive matter that the emphasis on aesthetic properties would make it.

When we emphasize the context of a cultural tradition these deficiencies are rectified. The painting is what it is in an artistic tradition. It does not stand in isolation as the bearer of isolatable properties. The recognition of a painting is certainly a judgement on our part but, again, that judgement has its sense or lack of sense also in the context of an artistic tradition. If the 'properties' do not stand in splendid isolation, neither do 'judgements'. Once we realize this, we can see why it would not make sense to say that we could appreciate a great painting if we had seen only one. At first, it may be difficult to see why such a supposition is senseless. One might think that the greatness of a painting is something which 'stands out' – thrusts itself upon us, as it were. But consider this suggestion a little more closely. When we say the painting 'stands out', stands out from what? Surely, from other paintings. We bring out the greatness of a painting when we contrast it with others. This does not mean that it is a comparative judgement in the way in which talk of 'the greatest pile' is a comparative judgement. We can speak of a small pile, a medium pile, a greater pile and the greatest pile. That comparison is simply quantitative. There is no qualitative difference. With a great painting matters are different. The great painting is not one of a kind. But this does not mean that the reference to other paintings is irrelevant. In a formal sense, the topic of a number of paintings may be the same – a certain landscape, let us say. In the great painting, what it does with the landscape can only be appreciated within the whole language of painting. It is when one painting is put alongside another that the difference between them can be appreciated. Some may be able to be more articulate than others about the difference. Indeed, in some cases, judgement may express itself in very few words, but be evident in an unerring selection. When one painting is put alongside another, one may say that one makes the other 'go away'. Similarly, we say that one painting 'cannot live' with another. Someone else may put the matter in words in such a way that we say, 'That's exactly how I felt about it'. At other times, we may fail to see any difference between one painting and another until someone teaches us to see what the difference amounts to. In short, if someone can put into words for us a difference that we have already seen, someone's observations may get us to see a difference that we have not seen.

My talk of putting one picture alongside another may mislead in some respects. It may make one think that in saying that a painting is great in the context of a culture, I was insisting that the recognition depends on an *explicit* comparison being made. Suppose that for many years one has been looking at paintings, often seeing them side by side in museums, art galleries, exhibitions, and so on. Now think of coming across a single painting and thinking it to be very good. One does not need to have a painting in one's possession before one can judge the new one artistically. The knowledge that one has of other paintings enables one to react immediately, even if closer inspection reveals more to one. One's judgement of paintings can only be an *informed* judgement in the context of an artistic tradition.[1]

What we have said about painting applies equally in the case of music and of literature. If I say that one composer's song-cycle is *deeper* than that of another composer's, I can only bring out what I mean by this in the whole context of a musical tradition. For similar reasons, we could not know that a work of literature is great if we had read only one. Its greatness would depend on a contrast with other works, not a contrast which has to be made explicit on every occasion, but one which must nevertheless exist.

I have talked of great painting, great music and great literature in order to emphasize the importance of a cultural and artistic tradition in understanding what we mean by aesthetic judgements. Such an emphasis may give the impression that I have not recognized that there are often wide disagreements in the aesthetic judgements that we make. I certainly do not want to ignore such disagreements, but their occurrence may mislead us. It is because of such disagreements that some have concluded that aesthetic judgements are simply matters of taste, and that it is impossible to discriminate between them. The centrality of the notion of artistic tradition in understanding aesthetic judgements should help to avoid that conclusion. It is easy to overlook the fact that the disagreements referred to are disagreements *within limits*. We might say that the only serious disagreement is informed disagreement. There can be discussion about whether the love poems of one poet are deeper than the love poems of another. But if someone asked how we know that Shakespeare's sonnets are greater than the doggerel of a local poet, it is interesting that we would be bereft of reasons if we tried to provide an answer. The question shows that the questioner is ill-informed; the query falls outside the context in which discussion can take place. Similar discussions can take place, say, about the music of Schubert and Brahms, but not about the respective merits of Beethoven and the Welsh composer Daniel Jones. I repeat: serious differences in aesthetic judgements and discussion of them takes place within limits.

There may be disputes about whether so-and-so is a great painter, musician or writer, but once we are no longer talking of greatness, differences begin to multiply. We often say that we can appreciate what others see in the painting, music and literature of so-and-so, although we do not like it ourselves. There will be cases in which we beg to differ. But other cases are not like this. Instead of tolerating the musical, literary or artistic preferences of others, we call them 'sentimental', 'romantic', 'indulgent' or even 'shallow'. As in the case of morality, these differences may remain unresolvable. There are also differences of another kind. Sometimes work can be looked at, heard or read in one generation or century in ways which become impossible in other generations or centuries. Sometimes we can appreciate, but not adopt these differences, but some may be closed to us. In all the contexts that we have considered so far, we have seen the centrality of the notion of an artistic tradition in an understanding of aesthetic values.

The notion is important for the understanding of tradition and change in painting. It is important to note that change does not occur in a vacuum and that new movements in art see themselves as correctives to their ancestors. They invoke artistic values or emphases which they believe have been neglected. This continuity amid change is an important factor in accounting for the assimilation of new movements in art. The children of the critics of new movements are found acquiring their works. When, in the twentieth century, an avant-garde emerges explicitly in the name of anti-art, it is significant that the children of its critics are not acquiring the work and the movement remains unassimilated into the history of artistic developments. These issues have important bearings on the question of what it means to learn from art, of what it means to speak of deeper and shallower treatments in painting, and so on. They are also important for the issue of the difference between the visual arts and nature, a difference which has much to do with the fact that it makes sense to speak of ideas in art but not of ideas in nature. But these are matters that I shall not discuss further. Similar views arise in music, with additional special issues. We can speak of ideas in music too, but it is more difficult to see what saying this comes to in music which is not opera, oratorio or a celebration of the Mass. It would be deeply misleading, even in these contexts, to speak of the music as *illustrating* themes independent of itself. Indeed, if that is what it does, it is more likely to be said of it in criticism rather than in praise. Great music does not illustrate love, joy, praise, death, and so on, but makes a musical contribution to these notions and makes them what, otherwise, they would not be. That point having been made, there is then great music in which we cannot speak of anything being 'said' in that sense. This consideration would lead to the whole issue of the relation of technical knowledge of music to musical appreciation. Again, these are not matters that I am going to discuss further.

In relation to literature, there has been much discussion of the intentions of the author and the identity of the text. Some philosophers and critics, in reaction against an over-emphasis on autobiographical details concerning the author in explicating a text, argued for a consideration of the text alone, to the exclusion of the author's intentions. But this view of 'intention' in literature is itself confused. Our intentions, in the main, are shown in what we do. If this is so, then an author's intentions are shown in the text. Whatever he may have wished to achieve − what he *did* achieve − is to be found there. But some critics have been sceptical about speaking of 'the text' at all, no doubt influenced by the possibility of different readings of a work. Nevertheless, we have said enough already to show that such disagreements, if they are to be serious, will be within certain limits. For example, we could not regard Shakespeare's *King Lear* as a comedy. But, as with other issues, I am not going to discuss them further.[2]

There are two issues, however, which I shall develop further. The first has to do with the sense in which art can teach us anything.[3] There have been two views concerning this which feed off each other's deficiencies. The first of these has been called 'art for art's sake'. Proponents of this view have wanted to insist that the arts do not stand in need of external justification in order to justify their existence. What the arts have to give us can only be understood on their own terms. So far, so good. The difficulty is that such a view insulates art from everything important in human life. We have already said that the arts do not illustrate hope, joy, fear, praise, death, and so on. That is true. But this does not mean that they are cut off from such features of life. If it were not for our ordinary hopes and fears, the fact that we exercise praise and blame, that human beings reflect on the fact that they are born and die, how could the arts express anything about such matters? We might recall what we said in the first chapter concerning mathematical signs. Without the application of such signs, the marks on the paper might just as well be wallpaper patterns. Unless the paintings, the music and the works of literature were connected with the hopes and fears, joys and despair of human life, they could not have the significance that they do. I have emphasized, hitherto, the centrality of the notion of an artistic tradition in understanding aesthetic values. It is equally important to emphasize, however, the connections between that artistic tradition and the general features of human life without which it could not be an artistic tradition at all.

It is this insistence, however, which leads to a second view about art, which has been called the didactic view of art. Adherents of this view see, correctly, that without a connection between the arts and human life they become decorative and marginal. The trouble is in how this connection is conceived. The arts are conceived of as *the means* by which we are taught something. But this leads to an external view of the arts: they simply *happen* to be the means by which these lessons are taught. This leads to the implication that we could have learned what we did without the arts. We could have learned it in some other way. This is exactly what adherents of the first view are afraid of, and which leads them to insist on 'art for art's sake'. If we could say of a great novel involving war, 'What it tells us about the war is such-and-such', would it make sense for someone else to respond, 'Yes, and what it says is true. I read it in the newspapers'? Wouldn't we feel that there is something missing, because on such a view the work of art is dispensable? In fact on this view, it is difficult to see why literature is needed at all. If we can summarize the lessons that literature teaches us, surely it must occur to us sooner or later that the summary is far more economical than the literary work. Why take five hundred pages or more to say something if it can be summarised in the form 'Its essential lesson is such-and-such'?

We can now see, clearly, why the two views that I have been outlining feed off each other's deficiencies. On the one hand, if we do not show a connection between the arts and any aspect of human life other than the arts themselves, they become, at best, decorative and, at worst, trivial. On the other hand, if we do emphasize a connection between the arts and wider aspects of human life, they appear to be no more than a contingent means of saying something which could be said just as well without them. On the first view, the arts seem to have nothing to say. On the second view, the arts seem to be one way of saying something which could be said in some other way. In both cases the importance of the arts seems to be unaccounted for.

Is there any way of avoiding this unfortunate conclusion? I think that there is, in a third view which insists both on the fact that literature has something to say and on the fact that literature is an indispensable mode of communication. It is here that the notion of an artistic tradition reappears as a central consideration. As we have said already, such traditions could not have the significance that they do were they not related to a wider context in the culture. If people were never sad or joyous, if they had no experience of hope or despair, how would stories which depend for their force on what they do with such aspects of human life have any force? If we sever the connection between art and the lives that people lead, it ceases to have any seriousness as art. But it does not follow from this that the story simply tells you something about joy and sorrow which you could find out by other means. On the contrary, if that were so, it would be a criticism of the story. If the story is a powerful one: what it says is inseparable from the mode of telling. This is the power of literature. It is not an illustration of our prior conceptions of love and hate, but, at its best, a contribution to them: so that although there could not be stories of love and hate if people did not love and hate, it is also true that our loves and hates would not be what they are were there no stories and songs of love and hate. I once heard an incredibly stupid response to this latter remark which was: 'Are you telling me I can't love unless I've read a book?' Of course, that is not what is being suggested at all. Literature, painting and music have had an enormous influence on people's lives which is both direct and indirect. Many people – probably the majority – may never have read great works of literature, but it does not follow that they have had no indirect effect on the ways in which we love and hate. The main point, however, is that literature can only have that effect – direct or indirect – by saying what it has to say in its own distinctive, powerful way in poetry, novels, stories or plays. The imaginative presentation that we see in these literary modes is not an accidental feature of what we are shown there, but is integral to it,

Yet, in reaching this conclusion, the sceptical voice that we have heard from time to time throughout the essay reasserts itself. It points out that we are taking for granted in all that we say *the possibility* of reacting to the arts in such a way that we can learn from them. But should this possibility be taken for granted? In the case of literature, for example, it has been argued that there is something irrational in our emotional responses to it. I want to outline this sceptical argument and some responses which have been made to.[4]

Suppose someone tells me of a tragic death in his family. I am distressed by what I am told and feel sorry for him. But, then, he owns up: I have been the victim of his rather cruel sense of humour. There has been no death in the family. The person said to be dead does not even exist. Immediately my distress and sorrow disappear. It would be entirely irrational of me to feel distress and sorrow when the state of affairs which prompted it does not exist. But this is precisely the case with literature. The depictions of people, places and events that we respond to with gladness, pity, sorrow and even horror do not exist. In that case, our reactions, surely, are entirely irrational.

There have been various attempts to meet this argument. The most extravagant of them is the suggestion that while I am in the theatre, for example, powerful depictions on a stage bring about a suspension of disbelief. I forget that I am in the theatre and think I am witnessing the real thing. Clearly, this argument cannot be maintained. If I thought I was really witnessing a murder on the stage, I would phone the police or try to prevent it. If I thought the place was really on fire, I would be getting out as quickly as I could. If I really thought I was witnessing a bedroom love scene, I would be a voyeur who had no right to be there. Such argument falls in face of these extravagant implications.

A modified argument may be put forward which, however, does not get rid of our problem. It may be said that while it is clear that in the theatre I am not witnessing a murder, a fire, or love-making in the bedroom, it is *as if* I were witnessing such events. But how does this answer our main problem? If I react to a death on the stage, as if it were a real one, it does not follow that I react as if I cry. No, I really cry. If none of my reactions to the death were like the reactions to the real thing, I would not be reacting to the death as if it were real. It has been pointed out that reacting as if the death were real is reacting in some ways as I do in real life, but not in others. I weep at the death, but I do not telephone for an ambulance. But now the original sceptical question reasserts itself: if it is admitted that some of our reactions are real, are not these irrational seeing that what prompts them does not exist?

But what is the difficulty? It has been argued that the sceptical challenge confuses two quite distinct theses. First, in real life, it is irrational to feel sad at a death if you know that the death has not occurred. Second, it is irrational to feel sad at a death in a story. Why should our assent to the first thesis make us think that we should assent to the second thesis? It is only because in assenting to the second thesis, we take ourselves to be assenting to the first.

The first thing we need to remind ourselves of – the argument runs – is that we *are* moved by novels, stories, plays, and so on. We have been acquainted with them from our earliest years. Why is it so difficult to understand that we are moved by them? The characterizations, although we know they are not real, are sufficiently real to really move us *in some respects*. In fact, if these reactions were not present, we would regard the people in whom they are absent or displaced as strange and eerie. Imagine a person smiling at some horrific scene, or laughing at the depiction of an atrocity involving a child. This is connected with the earlier discussion of the relation between literature and life. If there were not ordinary loves and hates, there could not be stories of love and hate. On the other hand, ordinary loves and hates would not be what they are without the stories. It is tempting to draw a false conclusion from this. If my emotional reactions to literature are due to the resemblances between what it depicts and real life, it may be suggested that what provokes my response is not in fact the depictions themselves, but real life all along. What really moves me is what the depictions remind me of, and what they remind me of is not further depictions, but real life. A depiction of a death reminds me of real deaths, and it is these that really move me. A depiction is an occasion to be reminded of the real.

This conclusion would lead us back to the confused didactic view of the arts that we discussed earlier, and to which the view of art for art's sake is an equally confused reaction. If literary depictions simply serve to remind us of similar scenes in real life, we can say that we can be reminded of them in other ways with far greater economy of expression, so making works of literature superfluous. What this leaves out entirely is the power of the literary depiction, a power by which we are emotionally affected.

Yet, in wanting to explain this emotional affect, it is easy to slip back into the confusions that we have already discussed. In order to press home the point about the similarities between art and real life, it has been pointed out that we do not respond to cardboard cut-out depictions as we do to the great characters in literature. The former are caricatures of life, whereas the latter are true reflections of it. This distinction is true, but its application is misplaced. It may be a sad fact, but it is one all the same, that very many people do respond emotionally to what is a caricature of real life. Such responses may be called sentimental, but they cannot be denied. The distinction between such responses and keener, more critical appreciation plays an important part, of course, in what criticism amounts to in the arts. But it is important to note that sentimental emotional responses are nearer to refined emotional responses than someone watching depictions of the human emotions *at any level* stony-faced, with no response at all. But the distinction between sentimental and true depiction can lead to the conclusion that because the latter is nearer to real life, it is that real life – which it is *almost* identical to – that we are responding to, and not to the depiction. This conclusion is clearly confused, for as we said at the outset of this part of our discussion, if we did think that we were witnessing real events in the theatre, we would not act in many of the ways we do there at all.

Once again, in bringing out the power of literature, it is easy to over-state the case. It has been emphasized, quite rightly, that we do not see a depiction in a work of art in a vacuum. We see it in the context of the whole work. Furthermore, the work has its place in a wider artistic tradition to which it may be sympathetically or unsympathetically related. It has been argued on the basis of these observations, however, that a powerful depiction in literature, in music or in painting, owes its force to the work as a whole. Others have pointed out the exaggeration involved in this, an exaggeration which would make nonsense of artistic criticism. We often criticize a work of art because the power displayed in parts of it is not sustained throughout it. The power of these parts that we admire, in these cases, so far from owing their power to the rest of the work, stand in contrast to it. In great works of art, the integration of its parts is often present. But what can be said of great works of art should not obscure what can be said of works of lower achievement.

In conclusion, I want to mention a topic which is difficult and important, and about which my comments are tentative. In the course of our discussion we have said much of the interplay between art and real life, emphasizing that our ordinary loves and hates would not be what they are without the influence of the arts. Some philosophers assume that such an influence must be a beneficial one, whereas the truth – surely – is that it is *mixed*. The nature of this mixed influence, however, is itself easy to misunderstand. It is easy to think that by the non-beneficial influence we mean the influence of the sentimental, the shabby or the vulgar in art, and that by the beneficial we mean the influence of good or great art. While I may not want to quarrel with what is said about the former category, the question I am raising concerns the mixed influence of good or great art. It is because of this that the arts have rightly been called dangerous. We cannot predict how the arts enter human life. To begin with, art is no moralizer. Sometimes, what in another context would be cheap and tawdry is transformed into something magnificent in a great work of art. We have mentioned the danger of thinking that art is real life, but there is also the danger of treating real life as though it were art. For example, imagine treating a person as a poem, wanting a person to have the kind of internal completeness that a good poem has. A great depiction of evil may lead to a fascination with evil. An admiration for novelists known for minute and delicate analysis of human relations, it has been said, leads to a more imaginative appreciation of our own relationships. But, surely, it may also lead to a disastrous over-scrupulousness, a constant analysing when trust and action are called for. These possibilities are connected with a wider important question which I am going to do no more than mention in this chapter: how learning from a person is different from learning from a novel. Put crudely, the novel doesn't answer you back. To be confronted by another human being, or to share one's life with one, is hardly comparable to spending one's time with a book, however great.

None of this is an argument against the importance of literature and the other arts, or the power of their depictions of scenes and sentiments connected with the lives we lead. It is simply a reminder that the very power that literature has is not that of the tamed moralizer some philosophers try to make it. But, as we have said, the desire, to tell stories, paint, sing, play music and compose is as primitive a desire as are our emotional responses to the results. The artistic activity and our responses are there like the rest of our lives, and they are mixed in character.

11

Believing in God

At the end of chapter 5, we recognized that one person may be an enigma to another. Although we emphasized the importance of common reactions in chapter 6, we pointed out that not all such reactions are shared by everyone. Realising this helps us to understand the moral disagreements between people discussed in chapter 8. We cannot deny that there are distances and differences between people. Nor can we discuss them very thoroughly without mentioning the striking fact that some people believe in God and some do not.

But what kind of difference is the difference between belief and unbelief? It is easy to give a confused account of it. For example, if we say that it is a disagreement over whether someone exists, we may think it is like a dispute over whether unicorns exist.[1] But there are obvious differences. For example, if I say that there are no unicorns, I do so within the more general talk of animals which includes familiar criteria for determining whether certain animals exist. We could raise the question whether animals exist within the wider context of our talk of animate and inanimate things. But if I say I do not believe in God, in what wider category does my denial have its sense? Suppose I say that I am asking whether there is a 'thing' called God. That gives the impression that just as there are unicorns, trees and human beings, so there are 'things'. But this is confused. We can ask what kind of things are tables or what kind of things are trees, but it makes no sense to ask what kind of things are 'things'. Unless things fall under some description, we have no idea what we are talking about.

The person who denies that there are unicorns shares the same criteria as the person who says that unicorns exist. But this is not true of the atheist. It is not that he sees what it means to say that God exists, but simply does not believe that he does. Rather, he cannot see what it means to say that God exists. He is not saying, 'I happen to believe that God does not exist, but, of course, he might have'. Rather, he is saying that God *cannot* exist, because to talk of 'existence' in this context simply does not mean anything. Atheism, then, denies *the possibility* of believing in God, for to believe that God exists is to try to say what cannot be said. This reminds us of the other examples of scepticism that we have met in this essay. Scepticism, as we have seen, is at its deepest always a denial of the possibility of sense.

Why has it been denied that talk of God's existence means anything? One of the main reasons is that when we speak of 'existence', we usually do so in connection with empirical objects. In this context, we know what it means to find out whether an object exists. We also know of the conditions on which its existence depends, and we know that one day it will cease to exist. In short, when we speak of the existence of objects, we are speaking of things that come to be and pass away. But when believers talk of God, it is argued, they want to speak of 'existence' without observing the conditions which give such talk its sense. We can come across a robin, we can come across a tree, but believers admit that it makes no sense to come across God in this sense. God is not an object. Furthermore, we cannot specify any conditions on which God's existence depends, because we are told that it does not depend on anything. We cannot ask how God came to exist, how long God has existed or when God will cease to exist. In short, God is not like anything that comes to be and passes away. Believers insist on that. But in this very insistence, it is said, they rob their words of meaning. We cannot see what it means to say that God exists.

At this point, two very different reactions are possible. On the one hand, we can say that the trouble with this argument is the

assumption on which it is based. It is assumed that if talk of God's
reality is to mean anything, it must be like the reality of things
which come to be and pass away. Here, the influence of the
language in which we talk of physical objects is enormous in our
thinking. It is as if we thought that God's reality aspired to be like
the reality of a table, a tree or an animate creature and fails to
make it. There is a paradox in the argument. On the one hand,
there is the insistence that we must be able to verify whether or
not God exists. On the other hand, there is the insistence that
anything the existence of which could be verified could not be
God, because it would simply be an object among objects and
God cannot be that. The atheist may say that this is no paradox. It
simply illustrates that trying to talk of God is meaningless. But,
surely, there is another possibility; namely, that we are subjecting
religious belief to criteria of meaning which simply do not apply
to it. The possibility of it having any meaning is ruled out because
we are looking in the wrong direction when we try to understand
it. If the language of our talk about physical objects is not relevant
to the language of talking of God, why subject the second language
to requirements appropriate to the first? The sceptic denies the
possibility of meaningfulness here, because he does not pay
attention to the possibilities of meaning involved. Why do we
assume that no matter what the subject matter – trees, money,
love, God – we can always draw the distinction between the real
and the unreal in the same way? How would we go about
distinguishing between a real and an unreal tree, real and unreal
money, real and unreal love, and a real and an unreal God? It is in
the different ways in which we go about this that we come to
appreciate the notions of reality involved. So we do not know,
free of any context, what the distinction between the real and the
unreal comes to. But if this is true, why should it not apply to
religion? Should we not explore *the kind* of reality involved here?
May we not find that, unsurprisingly, the reality involved is a
spiritual reality? If this is so, then finding God would be finding
this spiritual reality. Struggling to believe would be struggling to
find it. Rebellion would be defying or hating this spiritual reality.
This is the direction I think the enquiry should take.

I have not shown, of course, that philosophical enquiry should take that direction. I am simply indicating a possibility to which many philosophers do not pay serious attention. Why not? Why have the majority taken a very different direction in their thinking? On the one hand, there are those who are convinced that religious beliefs are meaningless. They stay within narrow limits in their thinking. On the other hand, they are encouraged to do so because theistic apologists stay within the same limits themselves. They insist on thinking that God is some kind of object. The hold of that picture is enormous. But what of the objections? The apologist admits that God is not an empirical object. How can the apologist admit this and yet retain *the same* assumptions? The answer is that God is said to be an *invisible object*. Let us see what saying this amounts to.

When I was a boy, I saw a number of films involving a character called 'the invisible man'. He was an ordinary man who had become invisible as a result of some kind of chemical accident. But he was there all the time, of course. He had a body. Others couldn't see it, that's all. You could certainly bump into the invisible man. He had to get around in the same way as everyone else. If he put on a hat, suit and shoes, you would see them, but you wouldn't see *him*. Apologists tend to make God the invisible man of theology. We cannot see God, but that does not mean that he is not there. God is like the invisible man, but with a further difference. God is necessarily invisible, because God does not have a body. God is a disembodied self. We are now reminded of the notion of the self that we discussed in chapter 4, that self which was supposed to be separable from the body, the passive recipient of sense-experiences set over against the world and other human beings. But we saw that there were insuperable difficulties in such a conception of the self. It is to this confused conception that the apologists I have in mind turn. It is an attempt to retain the picture of a 'thing' stripped, as it were, of all its inessential accompaniments. What we found was that so far from arriving at the essence of the self, such an analysis obscured and lost the conception of the self altogether. The apologist who turns to such a conception to find a foothold for

the notion of an invisible God is turning to a chimera. There is
nothing there to turn to.

Now and again, people saw the invisible man. Of course, if
they saw him, he was visible. According to the apologists, the self
is invisible, while what is accidentally ours – the body – is visible.
This reverses how it was with the invisible man. His invisibility
was his affliction. How he really was, was how he was seen – that
is, his real self – was visible. But sometimes it is said that believers
travel through life as people who have seen the invisible. But
when they see the invisible, it does not become visible. They see
the invisible; and they appreciate the invisible things of God. The
contrast with the visible, in this context, is with visible worldly
rewards. By the invisible is meant spiritual realities which turn
away from such rewards. To find these spiritual realities is to live
in them, or struggle towards them. In religious terms, this 'finding'
is called 'walking with God'. Philosophers seldom take this notion
seriously. As I have said, the picture of God as some kind of object
exercises a strong hold on them. But think of how you would
decide whether a person is walking with a dog, or whether a
person is walking alone. Now ask how you would determine
whether a person is walking with God. If they could but realize it,
for many apologists, walking with God is like walking with the
invisible man.

In the films, you only knew that the invisible man was present
because you saw other things. You saw a hat, coat, trousers and
shoes going about, but no human body. You saw a cup and saucer
rise from the table, the cup tilt and some tea disappear, without
seeing anyone drinking a cup of tea, or any strings manipulating
the movements. 'Ah', we said, 'that's the invisible man'. We
inferred the invisible presence from visible evidence. Some philosophers have suggested that this is how we come to know that
there is a God. We look at what can be seen, and we infer that an
invisible agent called God has been at work.

This argument runs into a number of very serious difficulties.
We must not forget its terms of reference. We have no direct
knowledge of God. We can only find out about God from what
we see about us. But this is the trouble. When we look about us,

148 Believing in God

it is hard to deny that we see good things and bad things in the natural world. There are wonderful sunrises, and devastating fires and earthquakes. So if we stick strictly to the evidence – as we must on this argument – the character of whoever is said to be responsible for all this must also be mixed. God seems, at best, capricious. Like the rest of us, God has good days and bad days. But, of course, this is not the God that the evidence is supposed to lead to. It is supposed to show us that God is perfectly good and loving. The argument that we are considering, which is known as *the argument from design*, simply will not allow us to draw that conclusion. We must not, and cannot, infer more about the author of nature than the evidence allows.[2]

The difficulties that the argument has to face do not end here. So far, it has been assumed that the problem is the mixed character of the evidence. But by what right do we speak of evidence at all in this context? If we see a watch on the seashore, we know that it must have been made by someone. That someone may be dead, but from watches we can infer watchmakers. Similarly, from the hinge of a door, we can infer the maker of the hinge. But from the bivalve hinge of a flower, no such inference is needed. Its origin is itself natural, making the inference to a maker not only unnecessary, but unintelligible. One way of putting the matter is to say that the argument makes the whole of the natural world artificial. It turns objects of nature into artefacts. This seems to miss the character of religious wonder at nature altogether. This is why it has been said that even if the argument from design worked, it would not lead to a religious notion of God. A designer is not God the Creator.

In a parable, which became well known, one philosopher asked us to imagine a garden visited by two people.[3] One, on observing the garden, concludes that it is visited by a gardener, unseen and unheard, who looks after it. But the other person, observing weeds and other features of the garden, concludes that no gardener would allow such things to happen. Each one sees and notes what the other does. They also consult others about gardens. But, at the end of the day, one believes that a gardener comes, and the other does not. What this shows is that the issue has ceased to be an experimental one. The reaction to the garden is not arrived at by testing hypotheses. It is not something that the facts will settle. For this reason, some philosophers have concluded that it does not matter whether or not you believe in God. In terms of the parable, one might say that belief or unbelief makes no difference to the garden. The facts in the garden remain unchanged.

There is one difficulty about the philosopher's parable. It is about a garden. Gardens are human constructions; therefore they entail gardeners. But that begs the question as far as nature is concerned. We are so accustomed to gardens that they lead us to look for unity and harmony where there is none. We would not be so disposed to think in this way if we looked at jungles instead of gardens. Jungles, with their leeches and tangled rattans, do not lead us to say that someone must have been ordering all of this.

Faced with the difficulties that we have mentioned, some apologists have argued that belief in God has been introduced in the wrong context. Belief in God, it is said, does not explain details in nature in the way the argument from design suggests. The reference to God, it is said, is not meant to explain why one state of affairs obtains rather than another in the world. It is meant to explain why there is a world at all.[4] Why is there something rather than nothing? But, now, what is this 'something' called the world? It seems that the argument that we are considering now treats the world as if it were some kind of great big object. But it is hard to see this if by the world we mean not only 'all there is' – a difficult notion in itself – but also all that has been or will be. The argument from the world to God is called *the cosmological argument*. It is an argument from the fact that *anything* exists, not an argument from an order perceived to be in the world. The argument suggests that no explanatory answer satisfies until we ask that last 'Why?' which leads to God. A chain of reasons leads back to God. But whether you need to ask a *further* causal question depends on the circumstances. Sometimes, no further question need be asked. As one philosopher put it, we do not need to mention grandparents in order to explain the procreation of children. So there is no necessity to go down the road which is supposed to lead to God as the final explanatory answer.

But there are more fundamental objections to the explanatory claims of the cosmological argument. It must be remembered that what it seeks to explain is the existence of the world; everything, not just the existence of this planet. We have already noted the confusion in thinking of 'everything' as one big thing. But, waiving that immense difficulty, what would it mean to claim that the need to examine it leads to God? If we see houses in various stages of completion, completed, in disrepair or in ruins, we can recognize the state that they are in because we are acquainted with the building and construction of houses. But we have no experience of the world which is in any way comparable. That being so, how can anything be said of the state it is supposed to be in with respect to its alleged origin? For all we know, it could have been the product of an infant deity, which has been left to run on uncontrolled once that infant had lost interest in it. Or perhaps it is the product of the dotage of a superannuated deity; a kind of basket-weaving among the gods. Who can tell? But if there is *no* way of checking any hypothesis, what sense does it make to speak of hypotheses at all in this connection? The position is not that we must remain agnostic about any hypothesis proposed. The point is that since *anything* can be proposed, the whole enterprise is shown to be a senseless aping of those contexts in which hypotheses are properly advanced and in which there are resources for their proper consideration.

So far, we have been talking about two proofs for the existence of God, the argument from design and the cosmological argument. It has been said that these proofs were never meant to prove God's existence in the abstract: rather, they were meant as replies, from within religious faith, to criticisms of religion. But if that is so, there is one awkward fact about them that has to be faced. Even if one said that the arguments worked, the most we would be entitled to say is that it is highly probable that there is a God. This is because what we are doing in the arguments is testing hypotheses. But if the purpose of these proofs is to clarify the nature of religious belief, it is clear that they fail to do so. The paradigm for religious faith is not the entertaining of an hypothesis which may or may not be established. Believers do not believe in a God who may or may not exist. They say that God is inescapable: in him, they say, they live and move and have their being. God does not happen to exist. God is said to be eternal.

This feature of God's reality is said to be captured in the proof of God's existence known as *the ontological argument*. According to this proof, we cannot say that God does not exist without contradicting ourselves. God, it is said, is the sum of all perfections. Existence is one of these perfections. I cannot therefore be thinking of God and deny his existence, since, if I try to do this, I can think of a being greater than the one I am thinking of – namely, a being who has all the perfections of the one I am thinking of – together with the added perfection of existence. I cannot say that God does not exist.[5]

In criticism of this argument, it has been said that the crucial objection to it is that existence is not a perfection. If I describe an object, I do not include 'existence' among its properties. Suppose that I say that an object does not exist. If 'existence' is a property of an object, a table which does not exist would not be the same object as a table which exists. If something is a perfect example of its kind, say, an island, there is still a question of whether the island exists. In reply, it is said that while an island is a perfect example of its kind, God is the sum of all perfections. But if 'existence' is not a perfection at all, this reply is of no consequence.

It has been said that what the ontological argument says is not that 'existence' is a perfection, but that 'necessary existence' is a perfection. The argument is not that God exists necessarily. In reply to *that*, it is said that this cannot be so, since anything which exists may or may not exist. Nothing that exists can be said to exist necessarily. But when it is said that God necessarily exists, this means that God is not a being which may or may not exist. It would be better to say that God is eternal. In reply to this it has been said that while God is eternal *if* he exists, that question cannot be put aside. Yet, can it be put in this way? By saying that God would be eternal if he existed, we introduce the very possibility of God not existing which talk of his eternity was supposed to rule out.

I think this objection is sound, but does it rule out atheism?

Does it mean that no one can say, 'There is no God'? I do not think so. We have seen that when the atheist says this, he is not saying that it happens that God does not exist, but that talk of God's existence makes no sense. So what we have reached is the following conclusion. When a believer says 'There is a God', he does *not* mean, 'There is a being who happens to exist, but who might not exist'. But when an atheist says, 'There is no God', he does *not* mean 'A certain kind of being does not exist, but it might exist'. The believer is saying that God is eternal, and the atheist is saying that there cannot be a God. As we saw, at the outset of the chapter, for the atheist, belief in God is senseless. Our question becomes: Does belief in an eternal God make sense? But what kind of question is this? If we say that the question does make sense, does that mean that we believe in God? That is a question we shall address later in the chapter.

Of course, if the belief in an eternal God does not make sense, we certainly cannot be believers. Furthermore, there is an argument which says that the belief can be shown to be senseless on the basis of something we *all* know to exist; namely, evil. If we reflect on the reality of evil, we shall come to see that belief in God is empty.

Sometimes, the argument is put in the form of a formal contradiction, which is said to be involved in religious belief once evil is recognized. God is said to be both omnipotent and loving. God can do something about evil, and wants to. But the abiding presence of evil, it is argued, shows that omnipotence *and* love cannot both be ascribed to God. Since evil is all too evident, either God wants to do something about it, but cannot – in which case God is not omnipotent – or God can do something about it, but will not – in which case he is not loving. Yet, the omnipotence and love of God are essential attributes. The presence of evil, however, is sufficient to show that they cannot both be attributed to God coherently.

How have philosophical apologists for religion reacted to this challenge?[6] For the most part, they have argued that the fact that God could do something about the evil in the world and does not, does not carry the implication that God is not loving. After all, they argue, there are times when a parent, observing the suffering of a child, could intervene, but does not, because the suffering is thought to serve a greater good. We say that children need to grow up by facing the consequences of what they have done, or by learning that this is the kind of world in which such things happen. But when we look at the sufferings of human beings, it would be grotesque to argue that these can be correlated with their moral character. This is the conclusion that we reached in chapter 7, when we rejected the view that life shows that it pays to be good. So let us put that argument aside here.

What, then, are the benefits which are supposed to come from suffering, benefits sufficient to explain why God allows it? It has been argued that God wants us to develop freely as individuals. The price of freedom is that suffering can occur, but it is a price worth paying. The trouble is that the suffering that an individual undergoes cannot be correlated in this neat way with the consequences of that individual's free actions. The suffering may be the result of what others have done. The argument then would have to be that my suffering is good because it allowed others to be free, and their suffering, caused by me, is a price that they have to pay for my freedom. The argument is beginning to look extremely peculiar because, in our dealings with each other, it is precisely circumstances such as these which lead us to curtail people's freedom. It would be no defence whatever against suffering inflicted on others to say that it was a free act on my part. If the suffering came under the criminal law, measures would be taken to curtail my freedom, perhaps for a considerable time, to deprive me of the opportunity of causing such suffering again. We applaud such interventions by human beings, so why are there not similar interventions on the part of God? Why does God not curtail the amount of suffering in human life? To this it has been replied that while, indeed, the amount of suffering does seem daunting, perhaps that it is only so from our perspective. Perhaps if we could see things as God sees them, things would not appear to be so bad.

This argument has shocked many, because of its moral insensitivity. Are we to say that the screams of the innocent are not as bad as they sound? Why should a distant view of what is happening count for more than that of the person suffering? In certain circumstances, we say that present stress is getting in the way of a balanced view but, in other circumstances, any such remark would be a gross impertinence on our part. Would we dare to speak of the suffering of those in concentration camps – men, women and children – in this way? The sufferings which come into people's lives, in various ways, often break them. Apologists have said that if God sent unlimited suffering on anyone, this would indeed be an irredeemable evil on God's part. Such suffering could not be justified in terms of the argument, because there is no greater good to which it could lead. The human being is broken under the weight of affliction. The apologist cannot recognize this, because he claims that God has seen to it that there is a correlation between our suffering and a desire to do something about it. Suffering prompts our initiative. The argument now sounds as if human life is an assault course devised by God to toughen up human beings. This is itself a picture of an immoral God presented as though it gave us a picture of someone with our interests at heart. But, of course, people are broken by suffering, and only blinkered philosophers would dream of denying it. Sometimes this is recognized, but in a way which retains the perversity of the argument. It is said that God cannot send unlimited suffering to any human being because there is a limit to what anyone can stand! This is to treat human suffering like an infinite series in mathematics. We say that in the series 2, 4, 6, 8 . . . the rule +2 can be obeyed to infinity. But imagine saying to Job, 'God has not sent you unlimited running sores, you could always have two more'. When we speak of people being broken by suffering, we are speaking of what *actually* breaks them, not of some abstract possibility. Furthermore, there have been circumstances inflicted on human beings which would break *anyone*. Faced by this undeniable suffering, how can it be possibly said to be *for* anything? The very suggestion vulgarizes us and blinds us to the afflictions which are there to be seen.

When attempts are made to make the evils that we suffer means to a greater good, these consequences can be seen to follow. For example, it has been said that without the sufferings of others, there would be no opportunity for us to develop moral responsibility with respect to them. But this is a vulgarization of the conception of responsibility. The sufferings of others are not *for* anything. Imagine the Good Samaritan saying, on coming across the man who had fallen among thieves, 'Thank you Lord for another opportunity of feeling responsible'. It has also been suggested that, with respect to our own sufferings, greater goods emanate from working through them, the greatest being mystical union with God. None of this gets rid of the most objectionable feature of the analysis; namely, the conception of life as an obstacle race devised by God. As for mystical union, this is a state achieved by very few. What are we to think of the economy of a divine plan which involves so many suffering for the benefit of so few? By now, at least, God surely can see that the price is too high.

Recognizing the difficulties involved in any claim that evil can be justified in terms of greater goods seen to be achieved on Earth, apologists have said that the greater goods are only achieved in Heaven. Since we cannot possibly know what these greater goods are, we must at least suspend judgement, or act on trust, until we see the divine plan in which suffering has been assigned a place. One reaction to this is to say that the suffering of a child cannot be made the means of realizing a divine plan; that to use a child as a means to an end, in this way, is itself immoral. To this it may be replied that this would be so if the greater good for which the child's suffering is the means did not include the child. But this is not so. The child's suffering, it is said is a means to a greater good *for the child*. In response, it might be said that what is wrong here is this very conception of what is good for a child. It involves the same perversity, it could be said, which led to burning human beings for the good of their souls. What stands in need of drastic revision is that very conception of what is good for the soul of a human being.

Looking back over the indictment of God and religion in face of evil, the conclusion can be expressed in this way: if we judge God by the standards of moral decency, God must stand condemned. God does not intervene in circumstances in which any half-decent human being would, and uses human beings as means to a further end in ways which are clearly immoral. On the other hand, if we say that it is a mistake to judge God by human standards, that God is somehow beyond the reach of moral criticism then, again, the consequences for religion are dire. There is a place beyond morality, beyond the ordinary language of decency and indecency, where God might be located, but it is the place we reserve for the monstrous and the horrific. So the choice is either to find God guilty by our moral standards, or to find him too monstrous to be worthy of ordinary condemnation.

Looking back at the course of the chapter, from the suggestion that to believe in God is to advance a hypothesis about the existence of something, to the efforts to express this hypothesis in the argument from design and the cosmological argument, and finally to the efforts to confront the problem of evil, by advancing hypotheses which would justify the presence of evil, one common assumption runs though all the arguments – that religion offers us an *explanation* of human life. Why should it be thought that to explain something always makes things better? If my child has died of an inoperable ailment, that will give me cause for great grief. But if I am told that there is someone who has a plan that arranged all this, that he could have intervened to save my child, but that the child's death was for some wider purpose, is that supposed to make things *better*? Surely, I am now confronted with even greater evils than I had imagined. The explanation has not made things better. It has made them far worse.

This brings us to the greatest divide in the philosophy of religion, but one which is not always recognized. The greatest divide is not between those who give religious explanations and those who give secular explanations of the contingencies of human life. The divide is between those who think it makes sense to look for explanations in these contexts, and those who do not. So you will find among believers those who are just as horrified as the secular critics at the kind of religious apologetics we have been considering. This is why many believers and non-believers feel a greater affinity between themselves than they do with believers whose religion seems to be reflected by the kind of apologetics that they advance. This allows for the possibility that a person's religious belief may not depend on, and be very different from, the apologetics that he or she is able to muster on its behalf.

Having given our attention to those who do look on religion as a form of explanation, let us look at those who do not. Faced by the vicissitudes of life, the blind forces of nature, unpredictable visitations of disease and death, the fickleness of human beings and the interventions of bad luck, people have asked, 'Why is this happening to us?' It is important to note that this question is asked *after* what we normally call explanations have been answered. The mother asks, 'Why was my son taken?' even though she has been given a full explanation of how he was killed. She is not looking for more explanations of that kind. If more were provided, she would still ask 'Why?' What she is looking for now is a way of finding sense in things, given all the explanations. That sense will not be a further explanation.

Some intellectuals would deny this desire for sense any place in human reflection. Ever since the Enlightenment, it is said, science has been freeing us from the vicissitudes of fate. But what does saying this entail? Did people speak of fate because they knew no better? Were they unaware of ordinary explanations? And if these explanations were provided, could they take the place of what is sought when people have spoken of fate? We have just seen that they could not.

I am not suggesting that everyone finds life strange and bewildering, but many people do. They are puzzled by limitations of time and space: 'I thought I had the strength to see that through but . . .'; 'I thought I could rely on that relationship and then . . .'; 'We had worked hard, the worst seemed to be over, and then look what happened'; 'We had everything to live for and then . . .'; and so on. In reflecting on these limitations of time and place, the thought 'If only . . .' keeps recurring: 'If only it hadn't happened just then at the time when I was ready to . . . wanted to . . . seemed able to'; 'If only I'd been born twenty years earlier when there was an opportunity to . . .'. Limitations of place are also evident: 'Why was I born into the family when those problems occurred?'; 'Why are my energies wasted in simply avoiding friction?'

Faced by these contingencies of human life, no explanations make any sense — not the kind of sense the questioner is looking for. Many philosophers — believers and unbelievers alike — see that nothing like a theodicy, an attempt to explain God's ways to human beings such as those we have considered, could provide the kind of sense that people are looking for. Yet many would say, nevertheless, that this sense cannot be found. All we can do in the face of the vicissitudes of life is to protest against them, even though we know there is no escaping them. We shake a fist at the heavens even though fate may crush us. That seems to be the only decent human response. Perhaps the people who respond in this way may even be prepared to speak of a god — a god of caprice.

What is not considered is whether the same vicissitudes we have mentioned, the same limitations of space and time, can lead people to speak not of a god of caprice, but of a God of love and grace. Let us recall the form in which the problem of evil is posed. The presence of evil is said to contradict belief in a God who is omnipotent and loving. It was said that either God is able to prevent evil but will not, in which case God is not loving, or God wants to prevent evil but cannot, in which case God is not omnipotent. But why should the problem be accepted in this form? The confusion is in doing just that. God does not have two attributes, omnipotence *and* love. What if the attribute God has is the omnipotence of love — not any other kind of omnipotence? Better: when we say 'God is love' we are not ascribing love to God, as we ascribe tallness to John when we say, 'John is tall'. When we say 'God is love' we are giving one rule for the use of the word 'God'. This, of course, does not get rid of the problem. It now becomes a matter of asking how some people, faced by evil and the vicissitudes of life, find themselves able to speak of the love of God.

Many philosophers will say that talk of God's love means nothing. It has no explanatory value.[7] If we describe someone as loving, certain circumstances would make us withdraw or revise the description. If we called someone 'loving', no matter what the person did, no matter what the circumstances, our talk, surely, would become empty. But this is precisely what seems to happen

in the religious case. *Whatever the circumstances*, believers speak of
the love of God. What can this possibly mean? In this question
we meet the kind of sceptical challenge which has arisen throughout the essay. What is being denied is the possibility of sense in a
certain area of discourse; namely, the talk of the love of God. It
may be said that what we mean by 'love' in this religious context
is different from what we mean when we speak of loving parents
or loving friends. The accusation, however, is that this claim is
simply an attempt to defend vacuity, obscurity and mystification.
But it would be dogmatic to say this *before* we look at the contexts
in which, it is claimed, talk of God makes sense. We must look to
those contexts in which belief in God has application in human
life.

We have already seen what happens in discussions of the
problem of evil when we think of God by analogy with a human
being. In terms of the undeniable fact of evil, God emerged either
as morally guilty or as a monster beyond the bounds of decency.
The challenge over the sense of 'love' places God in the same
context; namely, as one agent among others who has to account
for his actions: Why did God do this rather than that, and if God
did that or did not intervene to prevent it, how can God be called
'good' or 'loving'? But, as we have already seen, this is to mislocate
the place at which talk of God enters for many believers. It does
not enter as a form of explanation which tells us why one person
is struck by lightning and another is not, why one person returns
from the war and another does not, and so on. It enters as a
response to a world in which such things happen. It is not the
only kind of language that enters life in this way. 'It's fate' and
'That's life' also enter in the same way. After all explanations are
over concerning why this has happened rather than that, some
people are still bewildered about the sense of it all and ask, 'Why?'
'That's fate' or 'It's the will of God' are not explanatory answers
to that question, but they may come to replace the asking of it.
They are modes of acceptance, not methods of explanation. What
we have to do now is to give some indication of how talk of God
is a mode of acceptance.

It is essential in attempting this task not to falsify, or attempt to tidy up in any way, the vicissitudes of life which have to be accepted. The invisible things of God can only be given credibility if we do justice to the visible contingencies of human life. If we do not make the world believable, we cannot make the spiritual believable either. This is what is wrong with the solutions to the problem of evil that we discussed: in one way or another, they falsified the sufferings of human beings. In fact, they vulgarized them and our responses to them. If there is a spiritual response to the woes of the world, that increases not decreases our obligation to portray those woes accurately without denying their physical reality. The religious response that we are talking about, then, is one which concerns the sense of the *mixed* character of human life. It is not an explanation of particular events. Nevertheless, this does not mean, as we shall see, that it has no bearing on the significance that those particular events can have for us as a consequence of the religious response.

Consider, first, responses to the contingencies of nature. It is easy to ridicule the notion of the will of God in this context if it is thought of by analogy with human actions. What are we to make of those thunderbolts? God does not seem to be much of a marksman. His thunderbolts often hit the wrong target. The wicked often survive while the good perish. And what about all the thunderbolts which fall in the desert. What is God up to? Is this God practising before the real thing? Surely, scientific explanation makes reference to God irrelevant as far as thunder or thunderbolts are concerned. Could God thunder from a clear sky? Does God always need clouds to hide in?

But consider someone caught in a storm at sea in a small boat which is at the mercy of the waves. One minute the boat is thrown up, the next minute it plunges into the depths. It is not difficult to see how the colloquialism 'My life was in the lap of the gods' has application in a context such as this. But the believer's response is deeper: he is struck, in the storm, by a sense of the majesty of God's will. The believer is the creature in the hands of the Creator; his life, whether he is going to live or die, is in God's hands. Not that externally related to this storm is a God who decides to send it *in order* to test the believer's faith, or *in order* to give the believer a sense of the majesty of God (the anthropomorphic picture of God as an agent among agents, albeit the most powerful one). No, the majesty of God is revealed *in* the storm and the reaction to it. God's will is in the life or death of the person caught in the storm, in the same sense as it is in the storm itself.

The majesty of God's will is connected in this way, too, with wonder at the beauty of the world.[8] 'Beauty' is not being used here in a way that contrasts with 'ugly', as when we differentiate between different states of affairs. This is because love of the beauty of the world is a response to what is beautiful *and* ugly in the contrasting senses. It is a response to the world as a whole; it is a form of patience. The Book of Job is a famous example of what I am talking about. Job's comforters tried to make sense of the disasters which had befallen him by trying to correlate them with his character, or the misdeeds of his ancestors. The attempt was nonsensical. Job gives up the search for such explanatory answers to his natural question, 'Why is this happening to me?' Religious wonder replaces his question. In coming to see that his disasters had not been sent to him *for* anything, he freed himself from them, in a certain way. There are many ways in which a freedom of a kind can be achieved. Even talk of luck may bring it about: 'You were not to blame for the way things went. It was just bad luck.' But the religious response is deeper, since it includes that for which one is responsible as well as bad luck. The believer, like Job, ceases to make himself the central factor. The believer is not the centre of the universe; God is, whose rain falls on the just and the unjust. It is the wonder of this dependence which comes to Job and he becomes humble in it. He sees the natural world and its contingencies as gifts. Those things that we do not like come as trials. They tempt us back into the explanatory mode which makes one's self central in telling why this has happened rather than that. What Job comes to see is that explanations of that kind, although they were offered to him in the name of religion, do not exist. It is in this spirit that he is asked whether the rain has a father, whether he knows the treasures of the snow, and to reflect on the laying of the foundations of the Earth: 'When the morning stars

sang together, and all the sons of God shouted for joy' (38:7).
Wonder at creation is Job's salvation. It might be said that Job
ceased to think of nature as owing him anything. He came to see
nature as a form of grace. Hence he was able to say, 'The Lord
gave, the Lord hath taken away, blessed be the name of the Lord'.
He was able to say this, no matter what happened. But when he
said, 'Whatever happens will be the will of God', this cannot
mislead him about what is going to happen, because it is itself a
response to whatever happens. Someone might say, since whatever
happens happens, what does talk of God add to it? It doesn't
change anything. But this is not so. Our births and deaths are
necessary, but there is still the question of what we make of them.
Whatever happens happens, but there is still the question of how
we respond. Job's response makes all the difference for him:
wonder at creation rather than cursing the day that he was born.
Coming to God makes this difference: it changes the sense of
things.

Religion speaks not only of grace in nature, but of grace in our
relationships with other human beings. It is in this context that we
may show how God can be said to thunder from a clear sky.
Consider the case of a king who thinks that nothing can touch
him. No one, he thinks, can topple him. Suddenly, there is a
palace coup. His crown is snatched from him and placed on the
head of another. God, it might be said, has thundered from a clear
sky. The king has been taught a hard lesson: he may have been
the ruler of his kingdom, but he was not the ruler of destiny.

The notion of grace is central in the religious response that I
am considering. It distinguishes a religious response from a moral
response, with which it may easily be confused. Faced by the
contingencies of life, especially the way in which the wicked often
prosper and the good get hurt, a person may show a moral
resolution which may be described as a form of patience: 'No
matter what happens, goodness is not rendered pointless.' This
resolution may lead to a person facing even an untimely death,
forced on him as a result of his convictions, with moral equa-
nimity. This is something that he may have predicted with
confidence during his lifetime. All honour to such a person. But it

is not the religious response. There is one thing missing from it – a sense of grace. This can be shown by comparing moral resolution with one of the most well-known promises ever made: Peter's confident promise that, no matter what the other disciples might do, he would never desert Jesus. We know that when accused of being one of his disciples, he denied him three times. When did Peter deny Christ? The popular answer is: when he broke his promise. The deeper answer is: when he made it. His self-sufficiency was a denial of the grace which should inform all the endeavours of believers. Unlike the confident moral resolution, the believer promises by the grace of God. This again is a response to our well-known strengths and weaknesses as human beings. But although the response is general, in this sense, as in the case of responses to nature, it informs the particular. If the believer's endeavours are informed by grace, this will affect his view of forgiveness of others and of himself. When he sees betrayal on the part of others, he will say, 'But for the grace of God go I', and when he is guilty of such betrayal himself, hope of redemption is in that gracious mercy which he is invited to humbly accept, a mercy in which he is seen as something other than moral expectations alone would make him: a creature unworthy of, but in need of grace.

The religious mode of acceptance that I have been talking about, a form of love of God, is not a quietistic alternative to doing something about the evils of life. It would be perverse not to resist and change evil where we can. We are talking about what is still available when our best efforts are over. Knowing what can be changed and what cannot be changed, itself calls for wise discernment. The religious response is a response to our mixed lives. But there are features of those lives – institutional and personal – which threaten that response with counter-attractions and different attitudes. Obviously, those committed to a religious response are committed to resisting these.

In talking of giving an account of the religious response, I said that the reality of suffering must not be tidied up in any way. That is why I have left the hardest cases to the end of this chapter. We contrasted moral resolution with religious grace, and said that the big major difference is the recognition, in the latter, that it is only by grace, not our own merit, that we manage to achieve anything. But, now, the greatest difficulty of all must be faced. Does not the world have the power, through torture and other means, to extinguish in anyone this reliance on grace, the grace which informs the believer's life? In short, cannot the world kill or destroy a person's faith in God? Indeed, cannot it do this in such a way that we would say, 'No one could have withstood that'? Someone may say, 'God will see to it that this does not happen', to which one reply is to say that God has not. Another is to remind ourselves that we have already rejected as *religiously* inadequate, the notion of God as a 'Mr Fix-It' in the sky. So we must face the difficulty.

At the heart of Christianity is the figure of a crucified God. The idea that God could suffer such a fate is still repugnant to many believers of other religions. Yet Jesus, it may be said, dies an informed death. He says, 'Father forgive them, for they know not what they do'. A wonderful prayer was found in one of Hitler's concentration camps; it ended by asking that the love they had known should be the forgiveness of their persecutors. Perhaps not many could say that prayer, but it is a prayer which testifies to a death informed by love of God. Sometimes, by the time disasters or death comes, the world's persecutors have crushed faith out of a person. But if that person believed, knowing that such things could happen, we may still say, in this extended sense, that the believer embraced his death in faith. What we have appealed to, in these cases, is a religious reflection informed by grace. But what of the sufferings and death of children? These are limiting cases for many, since even if they appreciate the differences between the religious responses that I have been talking of, and spurious attempts to justify suffering in the name of religion, these differences depend on an appeal to religious reflection which the child obviously does not have.[9]

What, then, can be said of the persecution of children? Many adults executed in Hitler's camps made gestures of defiance as they died. But, for the most part, the children who were executed were silent. How could they be otherwise?[10] Whatever religion

says here, these deaths must not be falsified. Earlier, we said that
when we say, 'God is love', we are given one rule for the use of
the word 'God'. To witness absolute evil, as we do in this
persecution of children, is to feel at the same time that an absolute
good is being outraged. An absolute good does not triumph when
violated by absolute wrong: it suffers. It can offer no explanation,
no end to which the evil is the means. On such matters, it is
dumb. In the religious responses that we have been discussing,
God and absolute good are one. If absolute good can suffer, so can
God. The presence of the divine does not explain away the
suffering or justify it in any way. The divine suffers. It was said by
Jesus that to do this to children was to do it to him. The suffering
of innocent children is the suffering of God at the same time. In
Isaiah we read the following words: 'He was oppressed and he was
afflicted, yet he opened not his mouth: he is brought as a lamb to
the slaughter, and as a sheep before her shearers is dumb, so he
opened not his mouth'. But confronted by the silence of God, we
have seen many philosophers of religion react by saying: 'Well, if
he did not open his mouth we will, and give you here, as
elsewhere, the justification for this evil'. One way of understanding the arguments of this chapter is to wish that those philosophers
had not spoken.

In outlining certain possibilities of religious belief, I have not
been trying to find some alternative method to the traditional
proofs of justifying religious belief. What I have been doing is to
try to elucidate what these possibilities come to, possibilities so
often neglected in philosophy of religion. But this elucidation is
not itself believing. To believe is to give oneself to these
possibilities, to live by them. Put religiously, it is to give oneself
to God. Others may see the sense of the belief and rebel against it,
while others again, who call themselves atheists, may not see any
sense in these possibilities at all. Philosophically, my task has been
to show religious possibilities which provoke these diverse
reactions.

12

Behaviour, Explanation and Criticism

Looking back at the topics that we have discussed in this essay, it would be difficult to avoid their variety: philosophers' doubts about the possibility of knowledge; the possibility of finding knowledge in our sense-experiences; scepticism about the possibility of bridging an alleged gap between necessarily private experiences and an external world; the alleged differences between qualities which can be said to belong to external objects and others which exist only in our minds; scepticism concerning whether we are ever justified in talking about other human beings; scepticism about moral and political obligations; questions concerning what aesthetic values can be said to amount to; and scepticism about the possibility of believing in God. I hope it has also become evident that there is no one solution, no all-embracing system, within which the different issues that have arisen can be answered. A certain amount of emphasis has been placed on the notion of a form of life and the agreement in reactions to be found among us as human beings, but an equal emphasis has been placed on the fact that none of this is meant to ignore or explain away the differences and distances that exist between us. In this chapter, therefore, I thought it fitting to discuss intellectual tendencies to minimize these differences and distances. This can happen in two ways: first, in an attempt to explain them away; and second, to treat them, even when recognized, in such a way that they are not recognized for what they are. This second tendency will be explored further in the final chapter.

Let us begin by considering the first of the two influential movements in which differences between peoples are explained away. If distances between peoples are to be explained away, a major problem is presented by cultures distant from our own. These seem to present a situation in which there are deep divisions between 'them' and 'us'. But, it is argued, these divisions are more apparent than real. Properly understood, they can be brought under the jurisdiction of a common rationality which all human beings share. It is no accident that we all call certain cultures and the practices within them 'primitive'. We do so in relation to the more developed state we find in our thinking today. Mankind has gone through various stages of mental and intellectual evolution. If, therefore, we can now see the mistakes in primitive practices, we take no credit for doing so. If we were in their position, we would have indulged in exactly the same practices. We should honour, not despise our ancestors, since progress has been made piecemeal by the testing and rejecting of hypotheses concerning the nature of reality over the centuries. Had primitive peoples not advanced their hypotheses in the first place, no advance could have been made beyond them. It is only by rejecting what is false that we can travel in the direction of the truth. Of course, it has to be recognized that progress has not happened uniformly in all parts of the world. That being so, it is surely an obligation for those who have the light to bring it to those regions of darkness which still remain without its benefit.

This is the first powerful intellectual tradition that we have to examine. It is informed by an extremely important conviction; namely, that there is a difference between thinking that things are such-and-such, and how things really are. What we think – our hypotheses – must be tested against reality. Reality must be independent of what we think.

The next move in the argument is to point out the role of independent checks in science. Experimentation is extremely important. If we do not obtain the results which back up our hypotheses, those hypotheses must be rejected. Moreover, one has to make public the results of one's experiments. Thus we have the idea of an intellectual community characterized by the checks that it makes on any claims advanced.

How do primitive communities compare with this picture? We have to admit that their community, too, has its checks which are independent of any individual. For example, in the preparation of magic spells, or the observance of ritual dances, there are proper rules of procedure which must not be infringed.[1] A spell or dance may be rendered ineffective or discounted if these procedures are not observed by an individual. It would no more occur to primitive people to question the kind of procedures which govern a rain dance, than it would occur to meteorologists to question the causal character of the investigations on the basis of which they predict the weather. They may dispute whether this or that is the cause of rain in a given case, but they do not question that there must be a cause. Their whole investigation is a causal one. But is not the same true of the primitives? They may dispute over why a certain rain dance is to be ruled out, but they do not question the need to dance. The questioning, if it takes place, does so without the practice of rain dances. Does this mean, then, that the scientific and primitive practices are on a par with each other according to this argument? Not at all. We have not yet mentioned what is taken to be the fundamental difference between them. While there may be procedures for independent checks within each practice, there is this difference: the scientific practice corresponds to reality, whereas the primitive practice does not.[2]

There is a problem with this argument. As we have seen, we know what 'independent reality' comes to in the scientific context. It refers to the checks arrived at by experimentation. We know what 'independent reality' means in the primitive practice. It means the checks which govern the proper conduct of the rain dance. But the argument wants to use a reference to reality which transcends both contexts. Science is said to refer to reality, while the primitive practice does not. But this is confused. Neither science nor the primitive practice refers to reality, or, better: they neither refer nor fail to refer to reality. Rather, they are contexts within which we have distinctions between the real and the unreal. As we have seen, it is by looking to such contexts that we find out what the respective distinctions amount to. Hypotheses may be advanced in either context, but the contexts themselves are not hypotheses about anything. They give us the language in which hypotheses are devised.

How, then, can it come about that the primitive practice is said not to refer to reality? This comes about by philosophers ignoring the contextual differences and simply assuming that the primitive practice is a primitive form of science. Once this assumption is made, the inadequacies of the primitive science can be exposed in the light of our more advanced science. To illustrate how this comes about, philosophers have told a story which has become so familiar that many simply take it for granted. Primitive man, we are told, finds himself in a world he does not understand. He understands what he can control, but there is much that is beyond his control: thunder, lightning, the seasons, the coming of rain, and so on. In order to make nature less forbidding, primitive man personalizes nature. He puts forward the best hypothesis available to him. Since he is not in control of nature, he assumes that beings greater than himself must be in charge. This is *animism* − the belief that the world is peopled with spirits. As scientific knowledge increases, as natural explanations increase, the phenomena of nature cease to be attributed to spirits. Rain dances become obsolete because people come to realize that the rains come anyway, whether or not the dance occurs. Once we learn why it is that the rains come when they do, we cease to see spirits in the rain. We come of age and put away our primitive ways.

This argument does not survive scrutiny.[3] According to it, we have to attribute massive causal ignorance to primitive peoples. But this is hardly credible. They were skilled hunters and metal-workers, who had to have detailed knowledge of nature to survive. It is true that alongside these purposive, causal operations we have rituals, but can we assume that the rituals are regarded as causal supplements to these operations? In many cases, the surroundings, the context in which the rituals have their sense, show that we cannot. If the rain dances were ways of causing the rains to come, we could expect to find the dances when the rains were needed most. We would expect to find the dances during droughts. But we never do. We find the dances only when the rains are due anyway. According to the critics, this should make the dances superfluous. But this mistakes the meaning of the dances: they do not cause the rains to come; they celebrate their coming. In describing the dances as irrelevant we are mistaking celebratory activity for causal activity. To think that the dance causes the rains to come is as silly as to think that a woman who adopts a child in a ritualistic gesture of pulling out the child from under her clothes, does not know how children are born and thinks she has given birth to the child.

It will not do either to say that whereas causal operations really make a difference to things, celebratory activities are marginal and decorative. Let us consider some examples. A tribe may have rites which celebrate the coming of day. They do not pray for sun at night. They use lamps as we would do. These rites make a difference to the conception of a day, how the day is seen, the sense of how one is answerable for it, and so on. Compare it with how many of us greet another Monday morning! Can we speak with any confidence of progress and decline in these contexts, taking it for granted that we are on the side of progress? Consider also rites which surround hunting. Hunters may ask an animal for its forgiveness after slaying it. Crude explanations suggest that the hunters were afraid of being pursued by the spirits of the dead animals. Once they are rescued from these mistaken views, they drop the rituals of appeasement. But if we look closer at the context in which dependence on hunting loomed large in the life of a tribe, a deeper meaning suggests itself. The hunters have a sense of the mystery of life and hence of a life ended. This is expressed in the ritual. It shows their sense of the animal's life and the seriousness of ending it. Compare this with the mass killing of animals for food in our society. Can we speak of progress in our practices compared with those of the primitives? Rituals are not externally related to the activities with which they are associated, they are often constitutive of their sense.

It is important not to generalize from the argument that we have just presented. We have not shown that all rituals have the kind of sense that we have suggested in our examples. We do not have to choose between two general theses: 'All primitive rituals are mistaken hypotheses' or 'All primitive rituals are meaningful celebrations'. There is no 'must' about it either way. If we want to see what they come to, we must look to see the roles rituals play in the circumstances which surround them. Nothing that I have said is meant to deny the possibility of superstitious rituals. We are able to recognize their superstitious character by looking at the expectations connected with them. Some rituals may promise some kind of quasi-causal efficacy. Again, in all probability, as in contemporary religious practices, the picture will be mixed. While some celebrated the coming of the rain in the rain dance, others may have thought that the dance caused the rain to come. On the other hand, these admissions give no credence to the general thesis that primitive practices are mistaken hypotheses, understandable and justifiable at the time at which they were advanced, but superseded now by our scientific understanding. It is this thesis which obscures from us the cultural diversity which it attempts to explain away.

One further argument may be advanced in its favour. If primitive practices are not mistaken hypotheses, why should they fall so often when they come into contact with practices of more advanced societies? Does not their demise show that mistaken hypotheses have been corrected by better ones? This does not follow. Values associated with our practices may erode tribal values. For example, think of how the availability of large numbers of animals, modern methods of killing them and the profit to be made from doing so, will radically change circumstances in which animals are killed for the immediate necessity for food. It is not difficult to see how, under such pressure, a sense of importance of an animal's life, as expressed in the ritual in which forgiveness is asked of a dead animal, may be eroded or may disappear altogether. If this happens, one hypothesis will not have overthrown another within a common system of testing: rather, one set of values will have eroded another. Former practitioners of the ritual may call it pointless, but by the time they say this, the old values have already lost their hold on them.

It may be argued, however, that these conclusions are premature. They omit an important possibility with respect to primitive rituals. So far, the argument has shown that these rituals are not mistaken hypotheses. It has concluded too quickly from this fact that the rituals are meaningful celebrations. But there is another possibility, since although the rituals may not be mistaken hypotheses, they may be confused nevertheless. This confusion is akin to conceptual confusion.

Consider the kind of confusion that we may fall into in philosophy when considering the meaning of gestures – the gesture of beckoning, for example. We may think that the meaning is some kind of causal power accompanying the gesture. I beckon and *make* the person come to me. I point and the person goes off in that direction. What gives these gestures their meaning is the role that they play in our relationships with each other. Without these surroundings the gestures are lifeless. In rituals, words are often used which also have a use outside the rituals. But they may be brought into the rituals as if they could have *the same* meaning there, even though the surroundings on which the meaning depends are absent. It will seem as if the gesture of beckoning, repeated many times in the ritual, *makes* the departed one return. The meaning *will* then seem to be a power in the gesture. We must also be alive to the possibility that the beckoning in the gesture is itself the expression of wishes that go deep, not a quasi-causal means of securing their fulfilment. But rituals may contain radical confusion. This may be apparent in the ritual of the scapegoat. The goat, with a burden on its back, is driven into the wilderness. It is said to carry away the sins of a people. There are surroundings in which we speak of one person carrying the burdens of another. A father may carry responsibility for the misdeeds of his son. A tribe may carry the sins of one of its members. But how can a goat carry away the sins of a people? Here the surroundings which give sense to taking on the burdens of others are missing. In fact, the use of 'carry' in 'The goat carried away the sins of a people', seems to be the same use as in 'The goat carries a physical burden on its back'. And, of course, it *cannot* mean that.

What this conclusion allows is that there can be confused rituals, just as there can be superstitious rituals. But this conclusion does not affect the point that there can be no *general* thesis about primitive rituals. It is this general thesis that must be resisted. It hides from us the possibility of recognizing and appreciating the diversity of cultural practices.

The first intellectual movement that we have discussed may be regarded as a form of scientism, the assumption that all human activities, if they are to be called rational, must conform to the paradigms of scientific investigation. The second intellectual movement that I want to consider offers a paradigm of explanation of a very different kind. This time, the paradigm is not a scientific one but a psychological one. Its effect, however, is the same: it obscures from us the diversity of human activities.

We can appreciate the different emphasis in terms of the explanation given of primitive rituals. According to this explanation, the view of primitive man as an early scientist is far too intellectual. The root of primitive rituals is not in intellectual reflection, but in the emotions. In a world which he does not understand, primitive man becomes frustrated because of the thwarting of his desires. This 'thwarting' leads to a psychological crisis, a kind of breakdown. Rituals are aids to coping with such breakdowns. Mimetic rites convince primitive man that he has fulfilled the desires which, in fact, remain unfulfilled. But why do primitive peoples engage in rituals when they are not in the grips of such breakdowns? The answer given is that the rituals serve as a kind of preventative medicine. By engaging in rituals, people are given a strength which helps them to return to face the inevitable disappointments of daily life. On this view, the rationale of the rituals is found in the psychological crises of the individual.

Instead of examining this view in its anthropological context, I want to look at the most powerful form it has taken in our time; namely, psychoanalytic theory.[4] It is in this context that we find, again, a blurring of the different activities and movements that human beings engage in. As in the case of the psychological analysis of primitive rituals that we have just considered, so in psychoanalytic theory, too, we have the view that the explanation of cultural movements is to be found in the psychological crises of the individual.

The main thesis, expounded by Freud, is that the explanatory roots of the behaviour of human beings are to be found in infantile sexuality, the period from one year to five in a person's life. Tensions are said to exist between the male child and his father. The child envies his father's sexual relations with his mother. He wants to kill his father and to sleep with his mother. For a brief period, Freud believed that the child had actually attempted to murder his father. He also believed that the child had actually witnessed traumatic events, such as witnessing his parents having sexual intercourse. In the case of primitive peoples, because of his view that for them there is no gap between a wish and its fulfilment, Freud believed that these events had actually taken place in their childhoods. In the case of his own patients, however, it became obvious that these facts could not be substantiated. This absence of biographical confirmation did not worry Freud. He asserted that although no attempt to murder the father need have been made, every male child, during infantile sexuality, had harboured an unconscious desire to kill his father and marry his mother.

What are we to make of this claim? The psychoanalytic thesis is unfalsifiable. This can be seen if we reflect on the notion of the unconscious. The unconscious is misunderstood if it is thought of as an inaccessible region. The analogy of the unconscious as the submerged part of an iceberg is very misleading. 'The unconscious' refers to a pattern in a person's behaviour which, for various reasons, the person refuses to recognize. Clearly, there are limits to what can be attributed to a person's unconscious thoughts. What is ascribed to a person must make sense to that person. A person cannot long, unconsciously, to be a king, unless he knows what a king is. So there must be some features of a person's behaviour which lead us to attribute unconscious thoughts to that person. But how is this supposed to happen for the cluster of events in infantile sexuality to which Freud gave the name 'Oedipus Complex'? It would have to be established either by the evidence of children or parents. Most children, it is said, work through the complex as they grow. If they do not, neuroses will emerge in adult life. We cannot verify the events of infantile sexuality by asking the healthy majority. Having worked though their unconscious desires, they would not remember them. So we are left with the testimony of parents. They are not going to say that between the ages of one and five, they detected in the behaviour of their male children evidence which would lead them to say that these children wanted to kill their fathers and sleep with their mothers. The thesis is unfalsifiable. Under analysis, some people may accept the complex as the explanation of their neuroses, but this would not justify the general psychoanalytic theory.

It is an essential part of psychoanalytic practice that a successful analysis must have the assent of the person being analysed. In the case of primitive practices, this requirement was completely ignored. The beliefs of primitives were said to be irrelevant. But psychoanalytic theory should not even ignore cultural differences in family institutions. If such institutions contained important differences in parental relations, there would have to be, surely, a corresponding adjustment in the theory. But that is what we do not find in Freud.

Freud said that he recognized the difference between a neurosis and a social institution, but he never took the distinction seriously when he philosophized. Instead of recognizing the character and interests of these institutions, involvement in these institutions is traced back to the essential elements of infantile sexuality; elements said to be true of every human being. The objections to this are obvious: people come to new interests in adult life, interests which it makes no sense to attribute to a child. The view of psychoanalysis seems to be that the key to social movements is to be found in childhood. But a child is born into a society characterized by a wide range of movements and activities.[5]

According to psychoanalytic theory, the original form of energy is sexual. Other activities are analysed in terms of sublimated sexual energy. In strict terms, however, psychoanalytic theory can give no account of real development and change in human activities. On the one hand, the theory wants to claim that new interests in adult life can be explained by reference to sexual energy. On the other hand, if the word 'new development' is to deserve the name, it must be independent of such energy and not reducible to it. No doubt, when people come to new interests, they bring prior energies to bear on them. But this is a far cry from saying that these movements can be reduced to these energies. Further, it will not do to regard the various activities that people engage in as sublimated forms of sexual energy. There are no grounds for thinking that sexual energy is the only original form of energy. Energy connected with work is just as original. The argument against sublimation can be seen even when what is manifestly sexual is taken up in later developments. When Saint Theresa describes her experience of mystical union, she does so in manifestly sexual terms. She speaks of being pierced by a long spear, of the ecstasy of its penetration, and of the reluctance at its withdrawal. Any fool can recognize the sexual imagery. But what we have here is not a sublimation of the sexual, but a transformation of it. To see what that transformation amounts to, we have to look to the spiritual role of the experience in the life of the saint. It is this context which is ignored when people advance idiotic theses, such as the claim that mystical union is a substitute for orgasm in celibate females.

Other movements are not only not sublimations of sexual energy. The values that they exhibit may actually be at variance with the emphases we find in psychoanalysis. For example, it has been said that well known people such as Napoleon, Dean Swift, Joan of Arc, Oscar Wilde and Hitler, if they had had the benefit of psychoanalysis, would have been happier with respect to unfulfilled wishes in infantile sexuality. Let us suppose that this is true. Is it not also almost certainly true that these people would think that the matters they were engaged in in their adult life were infinitely more important than the resolution of childhood tensions? Further, the emphasis on resolving personal difficulties in psychoanalytic theory may itself be regarded as a low form of concern by certain movements. It has been said that what is liberating in scientific or artistic activity is the way in which you are taken away from a concern with the self. What is given primacy of place is the character of the work that one is engaged in. Of course, an individual may make original contributions to this work, but the innovation could not be what it is without the wider tradition – scientific or artistic – in which it has its sense. When psychoanalytic theory has ventured to speak of the values of such movements it has often produced a perversion of them. For example, appreciation of great art is analysed as narcissistic satisfaction. Because I am incapable of producing such work myself, I receive narcissistic satisfaction from the great art of *my* culture which, in this extended sense, allows me to possess the work after all. Such an analysis obscures, completely, the sense in which we may learn from a great work of art, the importance of which we discussed in chapter 10.

The major difficulty is that, given the parameters of psychoanalytic theory in Freud, no adequate account can be given of perspectives, values or attitudes which fall outside those parameters. The account which is attempted simply distorts them. Examples from the psychoanalytic treatment of primitive rituals illustrate this well. Consider what is said of the treatment of dead warriors by their captors. Among head-hunters, the severed heads of their enemies are the object of veneration in rituals. This is analysed as a desire to come to terms with an emotional ambivalence in the slayers towards the slain. They wanted to kill them, but having done so, also felt guilty about what they had done. The rituals are attempts at appeasement which have their roots in this ambivalence. What this leaves out is what is essential to the ritual; namely, the values of warriors. Compare the famous incident at Rorke's Drift in the war against the Zulus. After numerous attacks, the British garrison was reduced to a handful of men. Once again, the surrounding hills became lined with Zulu warriors, and the soldiers awaited the final onslaught. Instead, the Zulus raised their spears and shields in a salute to the survivors. Here was a salute from one group of warriors to another, a salute which transcends the difference between victor and vanquished. In the primitive ritual, is it not possible to see something similar? Addressing the heads, the victors acknowledge the contingencies of battle, that their own heads could easily have been on display in the village of their victims. They honour the dead. Here, too, is a gesture by one group of warriors to dead warriors, a gesture which transcends the distinction between the slayer and the slain. The point at issue is not whether my account of the ritual is correct. The point is that the limits of psychoanalytic explanation in Freud do not allow for *the possibility* of its being correct.

In the same way, Freud's psychoanalytic explanation does not allow for a wider diversity in our attitude to the dead than its parameters allow. The emphasis is always on emotional ambivalence towards the dead, especially towards the dead father. The sons mourn his death and yet, at the same time, are glad that he is dead. This emotional ambivalence is explained by reference to the Oedipus Complex. But this obscures further possibilities. In ancestor worship, the dead are considered so worthy of respect and veneration that some of them become household gods. Songs to them implore them never to leave the home again. Once this is appreciated, different possibilities emerge concerning rituals the meaning of which was held to be unambiguously clear by psychoanalytic theory. For example, consider the practice of accompanying the dead on a walk to the graveside. On the return journey, the last person in the procession, with the aid of a leafy branch, erases the footprints from the earth. In terms of coping with emotional ambivalence, this gesture is seen as coping with the fear that the spirits of the dead may come to haunt those who were, in part, glad to see them die. The footprints are erased so that the dead cannot find their way back to the homes of the living. But, surely, there are other possibilities. The walk is a last journey with one who was loved and revered. This walk will never be taken again. The erasing of the footprints is an expression of that fact – the expression of a last journey completed.

It is not surprising, given the limits of psychoanalytic explanation, to find the Christian Eucharist being given, by Freud, an analysis in terms of emotional ambivalence. In the sacrament we see the echoes of an actual murder, the killing of the father in the patriarchal horde by sons who were jealous of his sexual prerogatives. Once killed, the father becomes more powerful dead than when alive, and rituals of appeasement develop around him. In the Christian Eucharist the believers express their sorrow for the dead one. Yet, at the same time, in eating his flesh and drinking his blood, they relive their complicity in the original murder. This analysis ignores altogether the religious ideas which are to be found in the Christian ritual, ideas which are once again obscured by the limits of psychoanalytic theory.

Nothing that I have said implies that Freud did not bring new insights to understanding human behaviour in his clinical work. I am referring to the wider philosophical claims that he made. Further, it is possible to look on psychoanalysis as itself offering *one* way of looking at human beings and the activities that they engage in. But that would not satisfy its earlier practitioners who saw, in their practices, the fundamental explanation of all others. What we have seen, in examining this claim, together with the equally universal claims of the intellectual movement, which models its conception of rational behaviour on science, is that the diversity of human activity and practices cannot be captured by such fundamental explanations. As we have seen, the effect of entertaining them is to obscure or even deny the existence and character of other possibilities in human life.[6]

We have had good reason in the course of this essay not to minimize the differences and distances between human beings. As early as chapter 5, we had reason to comment on the importance of this variety. Despite the common reactions which mark our sense of the human, we also said that that sense involves a sense of the differences and distances. In chapter 6, the invoking of the importance of forms of life does not blind one to the criticisms which may be made of them. In chapters 7 and 8, we resisted attempts to impose a spurious unity on the multiplicity of moral viewpoints which exist, or to impose universal answers on moral disagreements and dilemmas. Again, in chapters 9 and 10 we saw the importance of recognizing differences in political and aesthetic values. It is the resistance to recognizing the variety in human activities which leads to the denial of the possibility of religious belief discussed in chapter 11. Finally, in this chapter, we have discussed the pervasive influence of two intellectual movements which try to give one fundamental paradigm by which the rationality of human activities is to be assessed, or one fundamental explanation in terms of which they are to be understood.

We may think that once we recognize differences and distances between people and the activities that they engage in, our intellectual troubles are over. We may congratulate ourselves on overcoming the tendencies which stand in the way of this recognition. But this may lull us into a dangerous complacency, since there is a way of recognizing differences which still does not allow them to be what they are. I want to end the chapter by exploring this danger and its consequences.

In the course of this essay, we have stressed the centrality of the notion of shared practices. For example, in connection with mathematics, we stressed that signs are lifeless in themselves. They have their life and meaning within mathematics. In an alternative mathematics they would have a different significance. There is nothing which makes us have the mathematics that we have, although we can give an account of how natural it is that we measure in our accepted way. Some philosophers have concluded from this that our mathematics is an *option* for us. But this does not follow at all. If we hear of a tribe who do not count – who operate with the categories 'enough' and 'not enough' – this may rescue us from thinking that the way we do things is the only *possible* way of doing things. But it does not follow that we have any option about counting, or about what we have to say if we are asked how many chairs there are in a room. We have seen in this essay how colours, tastes and smells get their sense from our common reactions. But this does not mean that we have any option if we see a red table, taste a bitter fruit or smell something extremely unpleasant. It is easy to miss the importance of our common reactions in forming our concept of pain. The example of a tribe who exhibit pain-reactions only to visible wounds may remind us of this. But this does not mean that we have any option about what we see in a car crash where people are lying around groaning or writhing in agony.

How does it come about that philosophers come to think that what we say in these contexts only has the status of optional or provisional descriptions? Part of the answer may be this: in examining the three contexts that we have mentioned – mathematics, colours, tastes and smells, and pain – we have concluded that there is no *one* account of knowledge which will cover these different contexts. The absence of a single paradigm makes it tempting to call the *different* contexts *options*. But to give in to this temptation is still to be in the grip of the very assumption one claimed to be free of, namely, that unless there is a single standard for knowledge, all forms of knowledge automatically have no more status than options for us. But, as we have seen, this does not follow.

It may be said that the options that philosophers have in mind are not the examples that we have just considered. Surely, it is argued, what they have in mind is moral, political and religious perspectives. They want to stress the optional character of these perspectives in order to rid us of the temptation of thinking that they are surface phenomena which hide an underlying unity. The philosophers want to emphasize that these perspectives are what they are. But are they recognizing this when they call the perspectives optional for those who adhere to them? I do not think so. We may regard certain drinks as pleasant, unpleasant, disgusting, and so on. Yet, we may have no objection to calling a choice of drinks optional, because, after all, it is only a matter of drinks. But we need not take such a view towards the plurality of moral viewpoints. The views that people do take will vary. As we saw in chapter 8, attitudes between them vary dramatically: from tolerance to open hostility. Some will regard views they disagree with as being all the worse for being a morality. So far as regarding them as being an option, they will say that no decent person should hold them. Philosophical accounts must leave room for these reactions, which is precisely what calling all moral views options fails to do. Indeed, if such talk is taken seriously, it is difficult to see how people take up moral views at all. Why should they have more importance than spinning a coin?

Recognizing differences may lead us into further confusions. We mentioned the most common of them in chapter 8. Because there is no standard independent of all moral viewpoints, or by which they can be placed in an order of priority, some philosophers have concluded that all such viewpoints are equal. We pointed out what was wrong with this argument. Having said that there was no common measure by which all the viewpoints could be judged, they promptly contradict themselves by saying that they are all equal; which is, of course, one possible result of a measurement that they do not believe is possible.

A further confusion may follow. Because philosophers stress the importance of recognizing differences, they go on to deny the possibility of eternal standards or absolute judgements. In this denial they may be doing no more than rejecting the *philosophical* notion of an eternal standard or absolute judgement; one which, as we have seen, is supposed to be independent of all moral viewpoints and to act as their foundation. But the mistake is to go on to deny the possibility of *any* talk of eternal standards or absolute judgements. *Within* a given viewpoint, there may be conceptions of absolute judgements and eternal standards. For example, the judicial punishment of the innocent may be said to be absolutely wrong, and some believe in God's eternal judgements. The mistake is to think that these moral and religious conceptions of what is absolute and eternal depend on the discredited philosophical conceptions, so that when the latter fall, the others are thought to fall with them. Again and again, throughout this essay, we have seen how philosophical theses obscure and distance us from the realities of our lives as human beings. This will be the theme of our concluding chapter.

13

Interrupting the Conversations of Mankind

Throughout the essay, we have discussed various threats posed by scepticism. These threats may be regarded as attempts to interrupt the discourses that we engage in.

In chapter 1, we discussed scepticism concerning the senses, a scepticism which seeks to stop one saying what, ordinarily, I would say without hesitation. I would not be allowed the certainty that I am sitting at a table, writing on sheets of paper. I would not be allowed the certainty that other people, if they came into the room, would see the same table and the same sheets of paper. Indeed, at its most extreme, scepticism seeks to cut me off from any certainty concerning an external world. I am said to be no more than a solitary centre of consciousness, locked in the circle of my own ideas. We discussed this radical sceptical challenge in chapter 2.

We may contrast sceptical theses with what we ordinarily say, but this contrast does not deter the sceptic. The sceptic argues that if we reflect philosophically on what we ordinarily say, we would no longer say it. For example, in chapter 3, we discussed the way in which we speak of what we call secondary qualities. We say that gold is yellow. But, we are told, this is a slipshod way of speaking. The yellow is not in the gold, but in our minds.

So far, the sceptical challenge depends on a distinction between my mind and its ideas on the one hand, and the external world on the other hand. How, from this mental starting-point, can I have any certainty about such a world? But with what justification can I regard this starting-point as myself? Am I to be identified with a pure consciousness? Others, thinking such a notion leads to mystification, suggest that the essence of my self is found not in the mind, but in the brain. But, as we saw in chapter 4, both suggestions seek to cut one off from the human neighbourhood in which I have my identity. In this neighbourhood, I stand in relation to other human beings. Scepticism seeks to interrupt this relation, as we saw in chapter 5. It asks me to take seriously the suggestion that I may be surrounded, not by human beings, but by automatons.

In many ways, chapter 6 is the most important in the essay. It tackles *the nature* of the sceptical challenges. We can appreciate it by seeing how we combat the threat of scepticism. Two contrasting reactions to scepticism were considered. According to the first view, a sceptical thesis simply rejects what we ordinarily say. It says that I cannot be certain that there are chairs or a table in a room; that there is an external world; that gold is yellow; that I have an identity; or that other human beings exist. In rejecting these sceptical claims, I am simply taken to be advancing contradictory claims. The sceptic says, 'You do not know such-and-such', and I reply by saying, 'Yes I *do* know such-and such'. The sceptic says I cannot be certain, and I reply, 'Oh yes I can'.

The second conception of scepticism gives us a deeper understanding of its challenge. If we think of our disputes with the sceptic as disputes over what is true or false, the disputes will seem like factual disputes with which we are familiar: disputes over whether or not there are chairs in a room, whether there are human beings in our vicinity, whether a certain object is yellow, and so on. But this misses the depth of the sceptical challenge. I am not accused by the sceptic of making a factual mistake about the chairs, human beings or colours. The claim is that there is nothing to be right or wrong about. What is questioned is *the possibility* of talking about physical objects, the external world, colours or other human beings.

The contrast may be put by saying that whereas factual disputes take place *within* a way of talking, the sceptical challenge seeks to disrupt a whole way of talking. The sceptical challenge is not an interruption *in* the conversations of mankind, but an attempted interruption *to* the conversations of mankind. If we and the sceptic were simply making counter-claims, the dispute would occur within an agreed common discourse. But the sceptic questions the possibility of that discourse. This is why the sceptic cannot be refuted by offering factual counter-claims.

The sceptic's challenge is a general one, but it is made to appear to be a particular claim. The criteria that we elucidate in combatting scepticism, however, are not criteria which settle what is the case. To question whether someone else is in pain, may seem like a dispute about a particular person. Is the person pretending or rehearsing? But to reject the possibility of talking of others in pain would be to reject a form of life which includes such pretence and rehearsing. To imagine someone cut off from such a form of life is to imagine, for example, someone smiling or laughing when hitting his finger with a hammer, or howling in agony when stroked gently. Such reactions, however, would not undermine our form of life. On the contrary, *our* reactions would determine the fate of such actions. The person exhibiting them would be marked out as the strange one, the outcast.

In elucidating the criteria which feature in a form of life, we placed great emphasis on reactions we share: reactions concerning physical objects, colours and pains. Such reactions account not only for agreement in judgements, but also for disagreements and negation. Common reactions also determine our sense of the human. All these reactions are, to a great extent, impersonal. We can take them for granted. But at the end of chapter 5 we emphasized that this agreement is not meant to deny the differences and distances between people. Because there is a widely recognized lower limit, beneath which is the monstrous and the unthinkable, this does not mean that there is an upper limit to aim at within an agreed sense of the human. We are often enigmas to each other. Here, the reactions indicate *personal* differences between human beings. The personal character of the weighing, readings, and priorities which feature in people's lives is also prominent in the chapters on moral, political, aesthetic and religious values which follow. The sceptical challenges do not take the form of questioning particular judgements, but of questioning the very possibility of judgements in these areas of our lives. As in other cases, we combat the scepticism, not by arguing over particular judgements or by offering alternative ones: our task is to elucidate forms of life in which such judgements have their sense. But this elucidation will itself have to include the various degrees of disagreement which separate people in those contexts. The distances and differences between people, so far from undermining our form of life, are characteristic of it in these respects.

What has been emphasized throughout is that the deepest sceptical challenges are challenges to *the possibility of sense*. That is why being in the grip of scepticism has brought some philosophers to the brink of madness. What seems to be in the balance is not the truth or falsity of something said in a conversation, but the possibility of conversation itself. But even when that possibility is recognized, it is possible to speak of the hubbub of discourses which make up the conversations of mankind in ways which fail to do justice to them. How does this come about?

One way in which to summarize the conclusions that we have reached is to say that they involve the rejection of *foundationalism*. Foundationalism is the view that all areas of discourse are answerable to common criteria of rationality. From what has been said, it ought to be clear that there is no antecedent norm of intelligibility to which all discourses are answerable. Nor can it be said that there is such a norm underlying their variety. It is therefore not the task of philosophy to make such a norm explicit. Yet, if this is recognized, is there anything more which can be said about the hubbub of discourses which make up the conversations of mankind?

It is at this point that certain post-foundationalist philosophers will not allow the various discourses to be themselves. Participants in the discourses, they tell me, must take part in an hermeneutic conversation.[1] This is said to be our cultural calling. The conversation, we are told, has the hope of agreement as its aim, a hope which persists as long as the conversation lasts. Actual conversations may have different outcomes. In a dispute, one party may admit to being mistaken or confused. In another dispute, those involved may reach a working compromise. In yet other disputes, someone, anticipating defeat, may withdraw to fight another day. But the 'agreement' sought by the hermeneutic conversation is very different from these ordinary, possible outcomes. It seems to be purely pragmatic in character. The best discourse is simply the one which comes out top in the conversation. Such a view by-passes all the serious considerations which make up actual disputes. Agreement, it seems, is said to be a good thing, no matter what it is agreement about. In a real conversation, it is not what is said which is determined by a need for agreement, but what is said, and what we think of it, that determines whether or not we are prepared to agree.

Because of the absolute value placed on the hope for agreement, other absolute values follow in its wake. For the post-foundationalist philosopher, a readiness to converse is good, while a refusal to converse is bad. The conversations of mankind are said to be informed by a common civility.

Saying this gives the impression that the discourses all contribute to a single conversation. Clearly, this ignores the differences and distances between people that we have emphasized. We did not speak of a single conversation, but of a hubbub of discourses. Some of these may not be on speaking terms with each other. Those who urge us to converse with anyone no doubt have in mind those situations in which the barriers of ignorance and prejudice need to be broken down. Strangers become friends. They forget other conversations after which those we have talked to are stranger than they were at the beginning. Sometimes, we should not talk to strangers. Sometimes, very little need be said before we break off the conversation. Again, in a serious conversation, its course is not determined by civility. Rather, it is the content of the conversation which determines whether we ought to be civil. Not everyone will react in the same way.

The post-foundationalist philosophers that I have in mind distinguish between normal and abnormal discourse. Normal discourse is defined as discourse which has, within it, methods for reaching agreement. Abnormal discourse is said to be created by someone who joins the conversation, but who does not abide by the standards of normal discourse. The term 'abnormal discourse' is used extremely loosely. The extreme example is said to be madness, but revolutionary changes in science are also given as an example. As we have seen, no matter how revolutionary the changes in science are, they are occasioned scientifically. This is what makes it possible to write a history of the subject. Arbitrary changes proposed by someone with no scientific knowledge at all constitute no threat and no seriousness. That is why placing madness in a spectrum of abnormal discourses along with scientific change is unilluminating.

Post-foundationalist philosophers also use the term 'abnormal discourse' in a very different sense. A perspective may have procedures for reaching agreement within it. But perspectives are now called 'abnormal' if they cannot reach agreement with *other* perspectives. Each perspective will define the others as 'the ignorant', 'our enemies', 'our opponents', 'those who differ', 'outcasts', and so on. But, according to post-foundationalist philosophers who invite us to the hermeneutic conversation, the different perspectives should *respect* each other. Because the perspectives have no antecedent foundation, no underlying foundation, and no goal towards which they are all moving, it is thought that this *must* be their attitude to each other. But, once again, given the differences and distances between people that we have noted, these will not be determined by the need for respect. Rather, it is where others stand which will determine whether we can respect them. As before, people's reactions will differ. Some will respect what others despise.

Those who advocate the hermeneutic conversation also say that an individual cannot give himself or herself wholeheartedly to any one perspective. But why should this be said? As we have seen, post-foundationalist philosophers deny that various discourses are answerable to one metaphysical notion of Truth independent of them all. But they conclude, confusingly, that the fall of this metaphysical absolute entails the fall of non-metaphysical absolutes. Within moral, political, aesthetic and religious perspectives, people may adhere to absolute values. If philosophers deny this possibility because they think that *metaphysical* absolutes are absent, this shows that they are still in the grip of the metaphysics that they think they have rejected. In order for an absolute to mean anything for them it *would* have to be a metaphysical absolute. But ordinary absolutes are untouched by the demise of the latter.

The same confusion leads to further recommendations. We are told that in the hermeneutic conversation, our allegiance should not remain with the dominant view. This, it is argued, would be akin to changing it into a timeless absolute. Therefore it is said that we must be ready to accommodate any novelty as it appears on the cultural horizon. We are told that it would be foolish to maintain our commitments once the majority have decided to move on to others. But does not such advice substitute conformity and prudence for serious commitment?

The post-foundationalist philosopher asserts that the various discourses that we engage in are not answerable to a conception of reality, truth or value, independent of them all. In saying this, the anti-foundationalist is correct. But instead of looking to the actual conversations that we engage in, to the values and commitments to be found there, the anti-foundationalist imposes external constraints of his own on our actual conversations. We have noted what these are: participants in any perspective must aim for agreement with adherents to other perspectives; they must be prepared to speak to anyone to achieve this end; if the end is achieved, agreement will mean no more than the dominance of one perspective in the conversation; all perspectives must be respected; no one must give an absolute commitment to any perspective, even the dominant one, since new possibilities in the culture must be accommodated; and it is foolish to stick to one's commitments when most people are ready to move on.

Those who invite us to the hermeneutic conversation claim to have rid us of metaphysical conversations in order to reveal the place of routine conversations in our lives. But this is hardly what has been achieved. Instead, we are given a vulgarization of ordinary conversations, a set of attitudes which seem to belong to the dilettante. But the dilettante does not really give himself to anything. It is ironic that such an attitude should be presented as a paradigm of what conversation becomes when freed of metaphysical presuppositions.

Throughout this essay, we have combatted sceptical attempts to interrupt the conversations of mankind. In doing so, we have attempted to allow these conversations to be themselves. This is what those who say that we must participate in an hermeneutic conversation do not do. They attempt to impose an attitude of their own on the differences and distances between people's perspectives in human life. That is what philosophy must not do. Furthermore, we have seen that the attitude advocated is one which actually militates against any integrity in discussion or commitment to values considered to be of absolute importance.

The foundationalist tries to give the different discourses in the conversations of mankind a metaphysical unity that they do not possess. This does not mean, however, that talk of the unity of language is pointless. But the unity is not a formal one. Talk of unity simply indicates that the various discourses we engage in are not isolated from each other. They bear on each other in innumerable ways. We can learn, develop and change in such encounters. The important point is that there is something to learn here. It does make sense to seek new understandings, to meet criticism, to change or to defend against attack. But this does not mean that we can abstract from the directions that people's lives take, and define, in the abstract, what the 'something' is which can be learned, understood and appreciated. The directions of those lives, as we have seen, will differ a great deal. But no matter how diverse these directions may be, there will be a difference between seriousness and dilettantism in the pursuit of them. This is why the hermeneutic conversation, in its import, is akin to the sceptical challenges that we have discussed: it threatens the possibility of sense and seriousness in our conversations.

In commenting on the various contexts in which sceptical worries occur, we have had reason to note that, in some of these, the agreements in reactions that we find there are impersonal; that is, we take them for granted in human beings. This refers to the agreements in reactions involved in our perception of physical objects, colours and other secondary qualities. In other contexts –

our relations with each other, our involvement with moral, political, aesthetic and religious values – common reactions cannot be taken for granted in the same way. The personal element is prominent in a way in which it is not in the other contexts. Yet, although reactions where values are concerned are personal in a way in which reactions concerning the empirical world are not, this should not mislead us about the impersonal character of philosophical perplexity concerning *all* these reactions. Those who invite us to the hermeneutic conversation think they have seen through metaphysics on behalf of others in such a way that future generations need not bother their heads about such philosophical questions. This ignores the depth of philosophical puzzlement. It is impersonal in that it may take a grip on anyone who reflects on the questions that we have discussed in this essay. Since the worries are distinctly philosophical, the road back from them is distinctively philosophical also. While travelling on that road, it is difficult not to impose our values and attitudes on the things and human beings that we meet on it. It is difficult to let them be themselves. Nevertheless, to achieve that, while combating the scepticism which threatens the possibility of sense, is the part that philosophy can play in revealing the variety and diversity of ordinary things; a variety and diversity which may itself be a source of wonder in philosophical enquiry.

Notes

Chapter 1   Philosophers' Doubts

1   For the conception of philosophy and scepticism with which the chapter begins, see Russell (1980), one of the most famous introductions to philosophy. For a classical source, see Descartes (1980).
2   For this conception of philosophy's relation to scepticism, see Rorty (1980).
3   For a discussion of drawing premature, sceptical conclusions from the variety and deviations found in sensory experience, see Austin (1964).
4   For the suggestion that scepticism can be dissolved by reminding the sceptic of what we ordinarily say, see Malcolm (1952).
5   For an argument which casts doubts on the claims made in Malcolm (1952), see Chappell (1961).
6   For a discussion of the various uses of 'know', see Malcolm (1963).
7   For the view that it is inappropriate to speak of 'certainty' where empirical propositions are concerned, see Ayer (1940).
8   For a discussion of necessity in mathematics, see Rhees (1970a).
9   For discussions of whether the contradictory of an empirical proposition makes sense in any circumstances, see Wittgenstein (1969).

Chapter 2 Minds and the External World

1 For a discussion of imagination and memory on which I have drawn heavily, see Holland (1954).
2 For a discussion of the scepticism which is latent in a dualism between mind and the world, see Warnock (1969). I have drawn heavily on this discussion.
3 For a critical discussion of the conclusions drawn in Warnock (1969), on which I have also drawn heavily, see Austin (1964).

Chapter 3 Primary and Secondary Qualities

1 For an influential distinction between primary and secondary qualities, see Locke (1971).
2 For a contemporary discussion of Locke's distinction on which I have drawn heavily, see Bennett (1971).
3 For a discussion of the various ways in which we distinguish between the 'real' and the 'unreal' in sensory experience, and on which I have drawn heavily, see Austin (1964).
4 For discussions of what it means to say that two people are having the *same* sensory experience, and the difficulties of saying that I could know the meaning of these experiences from my case alone, see Wittgenstein (1988). I have drawn heavily on these discussions.
5 For the striking suggestion that perception is a kind of dance, see Weil (1978), including Peter Winch's introduction to this work.

Chapter 4 Mind, Brain and Self

1 For a discussion of the difficulties involved in saying that consciousness could inform me of my identity, see Jones (1967).
2 For the view that I arrive at knowledge of my own experiences in the same way as I arrive at knowledge of the experiences of other people, see Ryle (1958).
3 For a discussion of functionalism, see O'Hear (1985).
4 For a discussion of the possibility that I am a brain-in-a-vat, see Putnam (1981).

5   For a discussion of 'brain alive *in vitro*' experiments, see Malcolm
    (1971).

Chapter 5   *The Self and Others*

1   For discussion of the suggestion that other human beings could, in
    fact, be automatons, see Wittgenstein (1988).
2   For a discussion of scepticism concerning other minds and difficult-
    ies involved in the acknowledgement of other human beings, see
    Cavell (1979).

Chapter 6   *Criteria and Forms of Life*

1   I have drawn heavily on the discussion of different uses of 'criteria',
    and the illuminating discussion of differences between Austin and
    Wittgenstein in this context: see Cavell (1979). I have also made use
    of the discussion of a form of life, and what rejection of a form of
    life would amount to. The distinction between critical questions
    about forms of life and bizarre projections from them is important
    in this connection.
2   For further discussion of the notion of criteria criticized in Cavell
    (1979), see Albritton (1966) and Malcolm (1950).
3   My disagreements with Cavell (1979) centre on the discussion of
    indeterminacy found in Wittgenstein (1988). For further discussions
    of these issues, see Winch (1987a,c) and Phillips (1992d).

Chapter 7   *Moral Possibilities*

1   For an attempt to link morality and self-interest, see Foot (1978c,d).
    For criticism, see Phillips (1992b,e). For a classical source, see Plato
    (1960, 1976).
2   For a famous identification of acting morally with acting from a
    sense of duty, see Kant (1981).
3   On the difficulties of defining the essence of a good action, see
    Winch (1972a).
4   For a contemporary discussion of the distinction between categorical

and hypothetical imperatives, see Foot (1978e). For criticism, see Phillips (1992c); for a reply to the criticism, see Foot (1978a); and for a further criticism, see Phillips (1992a).

Chapter 8   Disagreements and Dilemmas

1   For the view that what counts as reasons in a moral argument depends on their psychological efficacy, a view which is part of the Emotive Theory of Ethics, see Stevenson (1964).
2   For an account of morality in terms of principles and prescriptions, see Hare (1960).
3   For the view that not anything can count as a moral principle, see Foot (1954).
4   For the classical statement of utilitarianism, see Mill (1962).
5   For the view that if all the facts were known there would be no moral disagreement, see Foot (1978b,c).
6   On moral disagreement, see Rhees (1969b).
7   For a discussion of rights and obligations, see Melden (1959).
8   For a discussion of moral dilemmas, see Rhees (1970b).
9   For a discussion of the view that one can never rule out the possibility of a solution to a moral dilemma, see Anscombe (1981) and Beardsmore (1969b).
10   For a discussion of moral dilemmas and the principle of universalizability in ethics, see Winch (1972b). I have drawn heavily on this discussion.

Chapter 9   Political Obligation

1   For a famous discussion of the notion of a state of nature and the role of the sovereign, see Hobbes (1960).
2   For a criticism of Hobbes (1960), see Rousseau (1960). The criticism is that the analysis in Hobbes can account for necessity or prudence in obeying the sovereign, but not for political obligation.
3   On the idea of a social contract and political consent, see Locke (1960).
4   For a brilliant criticism of the notion of an original contract and prior consent, see Hume (1960).

5   On the notion of political legitimacy, see Weil (1987).
6   For a contemporary discussion of the notion of an original contract, political obligation, authority and freedom on which I have drawn, see Winch (1972e).
7   On the notion of a 'veil of ignorance' see Rawls (1971).
8   For a criticism of the idea of 'the good of society', see Rhees (1969c).

Chapter 10   Aesthetic Values

1   For the importance of artistic traditions, see Tilghman (1984).
2   For the relation of text and context, see Winch (1987d).
3   For discussions of learning from art, see Beardsmore (1969a) and Rhees (1969a).
4   For a contemporary dispute concerning our emotional responses to art, see Radford (1975), Weston (1975), Mounce (1980) and Beardsmore (1981). I have drawn heavily on these discussions.

Chapter 11   Believing in God

1   For difficulties connected with talking of God's *existence*, see Phillips (1974, ch. 10; 1993b), Malcolm (1964) and Winch (1987b).
2   For a famous criticism of the argument from design, see Hume (1947).
3   For a famous article which argued that the difference between a believer and an unbeliever with respect to the world is not an experimental issue, see Wisdom (1964).
4   For a cosmological argument, see the discussion of Aquinas' cosmological argument in Abernethey and Langford (1962). For criticism, see Kant (1953), Kenny (1969) and Phillips (1970).
5   For the ontological argument, see the discussion of Anselm's ontological argument in Abernethey and Langford (1962). For a famous twentieth-century defence of the argument, see Malcolm (1963b). For a highly original discussion, see Bouwsma (1984).
6   For a contemporary dispute concerning the problem of evil, see Swinburne (1977) and Phillips (1977). See also, Tennessen (1973) and Phillips (1993a).

7   For a well-known challenge concerning any difference that belief is supposed to make to human life, see Flew (1955).
8   For a discussion of religion and affliction, see Weil (1952, 1959).
9   For a famous novel which raises the problem of suffering, see Camus (1967).
10 For a discussion of religious belief and the Holocaust, see Phillips (1991).

Chapter 12   Behaviour, Explanation and Criticism

1   For a well-known discussion of oracles and magic, see Evans-Pritchard (1937).
2   For a discussion of Evans-Pritchard (1937) and the claim that whereas science puts us in contact with reality, magic does not, see Winch (1972c). For criticism of Winch, see Cook (1983).
3   For a discussion of language and ritual, see Rhees (1982).
4   For a psychoanalytic attack on religion, see Freud (1962).
5   For a criticism of Freud (1962), see Anderson (1962).
6   For a criticism of attempts to explain religion away, see the early chapters of Phillips (1974).

Chapter 13   Interrupting the Conversations of Mankind

1   For philosophy's relation to the hermeneutic conversation, see Rorty (1980). For criticism, see Phillips (1988). For an extension of the dispute, see Rorty (1991) and Phillips (1994).

Bibliography

Abernethey, George L. and Langford, Thomas A. (eds) 1962: *Philosophy of Religion: a Book of Readings*. London: Macmillan.

Albritton, Rogers 1966: On Wittgenstein's use of the term 'criterion'. In G. Pitcher (ed.), *Wittgenstein: a Collection of Critical Essays*. Garden City, New York: Anchor Books/Doubleday.

Anderson, John 1962: Freudianism and society. In *Studies in Empirical Philosophy*. London: Angus and Robertson.

Anscombe, Elizabeth 1981: Modern moral philosophy. In *Ethics, Religion and Politics, Collected Papers*, Vol. III. Oxford: Blackwell.

Austin, J. L. 1964: *Sense and Sensibilia*. Oxford: Clarendon Press.

Ayer, A. J. 1940: *The Foundations of Empirical Knowledge*. London: Macmillan.

Beardsmore, R. W. 1969a: *Art and Morality*. London: Macmillan.

—— 1969b: Consequences and moral worth. *Analysis*.

—— 1981: Literary examples and philosophical confusion. In A. Phillips Griffiths (ed.), *Philosophy and the Arts*. Hemel Hempstead: Harvester Press.

Bennett, Jonathan 1971: *Locke, Berkeley, Hume: Central Themes*. Oxford: Clarendon Press.

Bouwsma, O. K. 1984: Anselm's ontological argument. In *Without Proof or Evidence*. Lincoln, Nebraska: University of Nebraska Press.

Camus, Albert 1967: *The Plague*. London: Penguin.

Cavell, Stanley 1979: *The Claim of Reason*. Oxford: Clarendon Press.

Chappell, Vere 1961: Malcolm on Moore. *Mind*, LXX.

Cook, John 1983: Magic, witchcraft and science. *Philosophical Investigations*, 6(1).

Descartes, René 1980: *Discourse on Method and the Meditations*. London: Penguin.

Evans-Pritchard, E. E. 1937: *Witchcraft, Oracles and Magic Among the Azande*. Oxford: Clarendon Press.

Flew, A. G. N. 1955: Theology and falsification. In A. G. N. Flew and A. MacIntyre (eds), *New Essays in Philosophical Theology*. London: SCM Press.

Foot, Philippa 1954: When is principle a moral principle? *Proceedings of the Aristotelian Society*, Suppl., XXVIII.

—— 1978a: Do moral considerations override others? In *Virtues and Vices*. Oxford: Blackwell.

—— 1978b: Goodness and choice. In *Virtues and Vices*, op. cit.

—— 1978c: Moral arguments. In *Virtues and Vices*, op. cit.

—— 1978d: Moral beliefs. In *Virtues and Vices*, op. cit.

—— 1978e: Morality as a system of hypothetical imperatives. In *Virtues and Vices*, op. cit.

Freud, Sigmund 1962: *The Future of an Illusion*. London: Hogarth Press.

Hare, R. M. 1960: *The Language of Morals*. Oxford: Clarendon Press.

Hobbes, Thomas 1960: *Leviathan*, ed. M. Oakeshott. Oxford: Blackwell.

Holland, R. F. 1954: The empiricist theory of memory. *Mind*, LXIII.

Hume, David 1947: *Dialogues Concerning Natural Religion*, ed. N. Kemp Smith. Chicago: Bobbs-Merrill. Note Kemp Smith's Introduction.

—— 1960: Of the original contract. In E. Barker (ed.), *The Social Contract: Locke – Hume – Rousseau*. Oxford: Oxford University Press.

Jones, J. R. 1967: How do I know who I am? *Proceedings of the Aristotelian Society*, suppl. vol.

Kant, Immanuel 1981: *Grounding for the Metaphysic of Morals*. Indianapolis and Cambridge: Hackett.

—— 1953: *Critique of Pure Reason*. London: Macmillan.

Kenny, Anthony 1969: *The Five Ways*. London: Routledge.

Locke, John 1960: Essay on civil government. In E. Barker (ed.), *The Social Contract: Locke – Hume – Rousseau*. Oxford: Oxford University Press.

—— 1971: *An Essay Concerning Human Understanding*, ed. A. S. Pringle-Pattison. Oxford: Clarendon Press.

Malcolm, Norman 1950: The verification argument. In M. Black (ed.), *Philosophical Analysis*. Ithaca, New York: Cornell University Press.

—— 1952: Moore and ordinary language. In P. A. Schilpp (ed.), *The Philosophy of G. E. Moore*, third edition. London: Cambridge University Press.

—— 1963a: Knowledge and belief. In *Knowledge and Certainty*. Englewood Cliffs, New Jersey: Prentice-Hall.

—— 1963b: Anselm's ontological arguments. In *Knowledge and Certainty*, op. cit.

—— 1964: Is it a religious belief that 'God exists'? In J. Hick (ed.), *Faith and the Philosophers*. London: Macmillan.

—— 1971: Part II: 'Materialism'. In *Problems of Mind*. London: George Allen and Unwin.

Melden, A. I. 1959: *Rights and Right Conduct*. Oxford: Blackwell.

Mill, J. S. 1962: *Utilitarianism*. London: Fontana.

Moore, G. E. 1959: Proof of an external world. In *Philosophical Papers*. London: George Allen and Unwin.

Mounce, H. O. 1980: Art and real life. *Philosophy*.

O'Hear, Anthony 1985: *What Philosophy Is*. London: Pelican.

Phillips, D. Z. 1970: From world to God? In *Faith and Philosophical Enquiry*. London: Routledge.

—— 1974: *Religion Without Explanation*. Oxford: Blackwell.

—— 1977: The problem of evil. In S. Brown (ed.), *Reason and Religion*. Ithaca, New York: Cornell University Press.

—— 1988: *Faith After Foundationalism*. London: Routledge.

—— 1991: Beyond the call of duty. In *From Fantasy to Faith* London: Macmillan.

—— 1992a: Are moral considerations overriding? In *Interventions in Ethics*. London: Macmillan.

—— 1992b: Does it pay to be good? In *Interventions in Ethics*, op. cit.

—— 1992c: In search of the moral 'must': Mrs Foot's fugitive thought. In *Interventions in Ethics*, op. cit.

—— 1992d: My neighbour and my neighbours. In *Interventions in Ethics*, op. cit.

—— 1992e: On morality's having a point (with H. O. Mounce). In *Interventions in Ethics*, op. cit.

—— 1993a: On not understanding God. In *Wittgenstein and Religion*. London: Macmillan.

—— 1993b: Sublime existence. In *Wittgenstein and Religion*, op. cit.

—— 1994: Reclaiming the conversations of mankind. *Philosophy*, April.

Plato 1960: *Gorgias* trans. W. Hamilton. London: Penguin.

—— 1976: *The Republic* trans. A. D. Lindsay. London: Dent.

Putnam, H. 1981: *Reason, Truth and History*. Cambridge: Cambridge University Press.

Radford, Colin 1975: How can we be moved by the fate of Anna Karenina? *Proceedings of the Aristotelian Society*, suppl. vol. 49.

Rawls, John 1971: *A Theory of Justice*. Harvard, Massachusetts: Harvard University Press.

Rhees, Rush 1969a: Art and understanding. In *Without Answers*. London: Routledge.

—— 1969b: Natural law and reason in ethics. In *Without Answers*, op. cit.

—— 1969c: Responsibility to society. In *Without Answers*, op. cit.

—— 1970a: On continuity. In *Discussions of Wittgenstein*. London: Routledge.

—— 1970b: Some developments in Wittgenstein's view of ethics. In *Discussions of Wittgenstein*, op. cit.

—— 1982: Language and ritual in Wittgenstein. In B. McGuiness (ed.), *Wittgenstein and His Times*. Oxford: Blackwell.

Rorty, R. 1980: *Philosophy and the Mirror of Nature*. Oxford: Blackwell.

—— 1991: Solidarity or objectivity? In *Objectivity, Relativism and Truth, Philosophical Papers*, Vol. I. Cambridge: Cambridge University Press.

Rousseau, J.-J. 1960: The social contract. In E. Barker (ed.), *The Social Contract: Locke – Hume – Rousseau*. Oxford: Oxford University Press.

Russell, Bertrand 1980: *Problems of Philosophy*. Oxford: Oxford University Press.

Ryle, Gilbert 1958: *The Concept of Mind*. London: Hutchinson.

Stevenson, C. L. 1964: *Ethics and Language*. New Haven, Connecticut: Yale University Press.

Swinburne, Richard 1977: The problem of evil. In S. Brown (ed.), *Reason and Religion*. Ithaca, New York: Cornell University Press.

Tennessen, H. 1973: A masterpiece of existential blasphemy: the Book of Job. *The Human World*, No. 13.

Tilghman, B. R. 1984: *But Is It Art?* Oxford: Blackwell.

Warnock, G. J. 1969: *Berkeley*. London: Peregrine.

Weil, Simone 1952: *Gravity and Grace*. London: Routledge.

—— 1959: *Waiting on God*. London: Fontana.

—— 1978: *Lectures on Philosophy*. Cambridge: Cambridge University Press.

—— 1987: On the legitimacy of the Provisional Government. *Philosophical Investigations*, 10(2), April.

Weston, Michael 1975: How can we be moved by the fate of Anna Karenina? *Proceedings of the Aristotelian Society*, suppl. vol. 49.

Winch, Peter 1972a: Moral integrity. In *Ethics and Action*. London: Routledge.
—— 1972b: The universalizability of moral judgements. In *Ethics and Action*, op. cit.
—— 1972c: Understanding a primitive society. In *Ethics and Action*, op. cit.
—— 1972e: Authority and rationality. *The Human World*, No. 8, 19.
—— 1987a: Eine Einstellung zur Seele. In *Trying to Make Sense*. Oxford: Blackwell.
—— 1987b: Meaning and religious language. In *Trying to Make Sense*, op. cit.
—— 1987c: Who is my neighbour? In *Trying to Make Sense*, op. cit.
—— 1987d: Text and context. In *Trying to Make Sense*.
Wisdom, John 1964: Gods. In *Philosophy and Psychoanalysis*. Oxford: Blackwell.
Wittgenstein, Ludwig 1969: *On Certainty*. Oxford: Blackwell.
—— 1988: *Philosophical Investigations*. Oxford: Blackwell.

Index